W9-BAB-002

Praise for *How Not to Be Afraid*

"In a world in which everything seems to be imploding around us, I don't find it particularly realistic or helpful to be told that I should really be transcending fear. But I totally trust Gareth Higgins when he writes about his own fear and how it's actually possible to transform it into something powerful, something capable of healing us and the world."

—Nadia Bolz-Weber, author of *Shameless*;
Accidental Saints; and *Pastrix*

"It is easy to say 'Do not be afraid,' but it is difficult to live it. In this book, Gareth Higgins brings us on a journey from fear to courage, from being afraid to not staying afraid, from defensiveness to an imagination about what justice might look like in private and public. Gareth Higgins is a friend. This book is too."

—Pádraig Ó Tuama, writer, poet, Theologian-in-Residence
at On Being, and author of *In the Shelter*

"In *How Not to Be Afraid*, Gareth Higgins doesn't dismiss the very real fear we feel, but instead invites us into stories and practices that offer us ways to process our feelings and experiences and bravely cultivate substantial, generative love. This book is a much-needed resource for skill-building through our fear and trauma so we might create the belonging and communities we desire."

—Micky ScottBey Jones, the Justice Doula, director of healing
and resilience initiatives with Faith Matters Network

"Through his brilliance as a storyteller, Gareth Higgins has allowed us simple but deep insights into the possibility of managing the debilitating emotion of fear. By bearing his soul-exhausting experience with fear, he allows us to take our own hero's journey to find our way through."

—Dr. James McLeary, former CEO of Inside Circle
Foundation and executive producer of the
award-winning documentary *The Work*

"Gareth Higgins spent years feeling trapped in fear, but you wouldn't guess that about him now. He has worked out an escape route from fear, and he was kind enough to write down each turn along the journey. This practical book makes it a lot easier for each of us to find a way to not be afraid."

—David Wilcox, storyteller, singer, and songwriter behind *The View from the Edge*

"Gareth Higgins's book reminds us that it's never too late to sit down for a cup of tea with your shadows and your fears. Like old friends, you'll have plenty to talk about."

—Rodrigo Dorfman, award-winning filmmaker, multimedia producer, and visual storyteller

"I'm so happy this beautiful book is here. Gareth Higgins has a certain rare magic as a writer and human being. This book will touch you and help you overcome fear, live with courage and creativity, and find meaning on this frightened planet."

—Brian D. McLaren, author of *Faith After Doubt* and *The Galápagos Islands: A Spiritual Journey*

"This storytelling is really captivating! The depth I sensed in the writing touched and opened my heart. I'm already thinking of many people I want to give this book to. I'm grateful Gareth poured his precious time and singular abilities into this work."

—Mark Silver, founder of Heart of Business

"This is a book written exactly for these challenging times. I don't remember ever reading a book so creatively structured."

—Nancy Hastings Sehested, prison chaplain and pastor

"Uniquely crafted! Sure to be an important, transformational read for a lot of people."

—Tyler McCabe, former program director at Image Journal

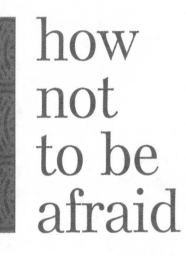

how
not
to be
afraid

how
not
to be
afraid

SEVEN WAYS TO LIVE WHEN
EVERYTHING SEEMS TERRIFYING

gareth higgins

foreword by kathleen norris

Broadleaf Books
Minneapolis

HOW NOT TO BE AFRAID
Seven Ways to Live When Everything Seems Terrifying

Cover design by Juicebox

Print ISBN: 978-1-5064-6903-4
eBook ISBN: 978-1-5064-6904-1

for brian ammons,

who once woke me up from a nightmare

and said, "You're OK. You're OK.

You have what you need."

And he was right.

I have learned over the years that when one's mind is made up, this diminishes fear; knowing what must be done does away with fear.

—Rosa Parks

contents

foreword

"YOUR ENJOYMENT OF the world is never right, till every morning you awake in heaven." Not many of us can match the abandon of the seventeenth-century British poet Thomas Traherne, but he lets us know we have an option: to embrace gratitude so fully that it eclipses our anxieties and fears.

Lest we dismiss Traherne as naive or foolish, consider that his was a remarkably unstable era: a violent civil war and the execution of the king, followed by the brutal dictatorship of Oliver Cromwell. Social unrest eased when Traherne was twenty-four and newly ordained as an Anglican priest, but five years later, the bubonic plague struck London, killing thousands and shutting down all trade and social life. Imagine the terror of not knowing what had caused the disease, what might cure it, or how long it would last.

And yet we find Thomas Traherne waking every morning in heaven. His religious faith no doubt helped him, but the kind of gratitude he exudes does not require it. It does require a realistic assessment of our fears.

Now we have a book to help us with that: *How Not to Be Afraid*, a wholehearted blend of memoir and practical suggestions for coping with fear. It is a necessary book at a time when so many have so much to fear and when fear is being manipulated for political gain. Gareth Higgins examines the full range of human anxieties, from personal feelings of shame and exclusion to concerns about social upheaval. He firmly rejects the notion that violence is needed to conquer fear and restore order.

I became a friend of Gareth when he invited me to one of his annual retreats in Northern Ireland. There I learned more about the terrors he experienced growing up during the Troubles. But I also learned about the peacemaking efforts that he and many others are engaged in there in the hope of transforming their society for the better.

I confess that I don't like self-help books. They typically offer a false sense of security, suggesting that we can control our lives with cheerful thoughts and a list of dos and don'ts. This book is an altogether different animal. It's a gentle, open invitation, full of hospitable storytelling that allows us to find ourselves in its pages. As we read about how Gareth has faced terror in his life, we are challenged to reflect on our own fears and to imagine a way to a better self, a better story.

God knows we need it. We may be hardwired to fear genuine danger. But all too often, we let it imprison us until, as Gareth points out, it becomes self-defeating. I once witnessed a dear friend pacing, wringing her hands, and grinding her teeth, fretting about her daughter who was driving home for Thanksgiving from a college two hundred miles away. When at last the girl entered the house, there were hugs and tears and laughter. But within minutes, my friend was grinding her teeth again and wringing her hands. "What's wrong?" I asked, and she replied, "Now I have to worry about how to get her back safely."

Our fears can be a spiritual short circuit, as they were for my friend: preventing us from being fully present, even to those we love. But Gareth knows there is another way, and he provides valuable insight into the difference between debilitating fear and a holy fear that gives us courage. Naming and facing our fears can open us to acts of great compassion.

I think of the Cistercian women who have chosen to re-main in Venezuela despite the worsening chaos there. Taking a stand for kindness in the face of violence and adversity, they share with their neighbors in ever-increasing deprivations, and they do what they can for the people who come to them seeking food, clothing, shoes, and medicine. A recent photograph shows the women smiling broadly. They are living the story they were called to live, cultivating peace in difficult circumstances. If they encountered Gareth's claim that "the authority to tell a story may be more powerful than the ability to launch missiles," I imagine they would laugh and say, "Of course!"

To choose not to fear in the face of danger can make us not only grateful but boldly prophetic—which brings me back to Thomas Traherne. "You never enjoy the world aright till the sea itself floweth in your veins," he wrote, "till you are clothed with the heavens, and crowned with the stars." What he could only imagine we now know to be true: human blood has the same chemical composition as seawater, and every atom in our bodies was once inside a star.

Thanks to the Hubble Telescope, we are the first people able to see our home in full, a mostly blue and beautiful orb in the dark of space. There is, in our fears, a better story; let this book help you find it.

—Kathleen Norris, author of *Journey: New & Selected Poems, Dakota, The Cloister Walk,* and *Acedia & Me*

preface

AS I WAS finishing the final draft of this book, you and I were living in the midst of crises. The existential threat of climate change loomed, the COVID-19 pandemic had taken the lives of an unimaginable number of people, and authoritarianism continued to assert that some lives are worth more than others. The lockdown response to COVID-19 left many of us feeling depressed in both our hearts and our bank balances. The world we thought we knew was revealed to be broken.

Yet at the same time that a pandemic was underway, another global movement was unfolding, this one beautiful and life-giving and perhaps even offering an antidote to the other crises. It was a movement of courage and creativity in which masses of people discovered and lived into an interdependent relationship with the ecosystem and with humans locally and around the world. It believed in the vision of beloved community, it nonviolently opposed supremacist narratives and aggressive individualism, and it acted for a more equitable, peaceful, beautiful society. Sometimes this movement looked like a dam bursting, sometimes it seemed like poetry, and no matter what mistakes or pain happened on its fringes, the animating heart of the movement embodied active hope. By the time you read this book, your world may look very different. Or not.

People have been predicting the end of the world since shortly after we started telling stories, and prophecies of future utopia seem just as prevalent. Whether things are getting better or worse depends on the vantage point and the measures of what concerns us. I have found it more helpful to imagine that each moment brings both gifts and challenges. No life-giving purpose is served by overstating the challenges we face or especially by panicking about them. Hiding from the world's pain obviously doesn't help either. On the other hand, overstating "progress" can have the effect of blinding us to the ways in which some things really have changed for the better. We also need to learn about the things that humans *can actually do* to help make them better still. But you don't have to be in denial about real suffering to see the amazing possibilities and goodness of a moment in which interdependence among humans and with the ecosystem is more loudly, widely, and creatively expressed than ever. And it's possible, to be honest, to face the obstacles to a more whole way of being without taking on the mantle of a prophet of doom. People are broken, so broken things will occur. Yet people are capable of more, and better, than we often credit. If we pay attention to what is most real, people will continue to awaken to overcome the power of selfishness. Many of the world's broken ways of being will be healed with more whole ways. The interdependency of relationships among humans and within the ecosystem will be more honored, inequities and other injustices will be faced and overcome by the vision of beloved community, and retribution will give way to creativity. Some things will keep breaking, yet amid their wreckage, healing will accelerate. How much we experience of the healing will depend on the story we tell—perhaps, especially, on the story we tell about fear.

Whatever else has taken place since I wrote these words, I offer them still in the active hope that the history of fear and of people who have learned to transform or even repair its wounds has much to teach us. Of course our social locations shape how we experience fear and the external resources most easily available to us. It is more demanding to walk through a racist context as a person of color, through a heterosexist context as an LGBTQ+ person, and through a patriarchal context as a woman. My race, gender, socioeconomic status, sexual orientation, educational background, and citizenship grant me some unearned privileges, and there are also some places where I may be seen to begin at a disadvantage. I'm more privileged than most, and I carry some burdens too. The responsibility demanded of privilege is to serve. The invitation in the places we lack privilege is to seek support in interdependent community. I am both challenged and inspired by adrienne maree brown's mantra: "Where we are born into privilege, we are charged with dismantling any myth of supremacy. Where we are born into struggle, we are charged with claiming our dignity, joy, and liberation." This book outlines some steps we might take toward overcoming unnecessary and debilitating fear, toward serving from our privilege, and toward repair of our lack.

One of the most important lessons embodied by the most visible advocates of beloved community—from Jesus to Rosa Parks, from John Lewis to Bayard Rustin—is that overcoming fear is mostly an inside job, not entirely dependent on personal or political circumstances. What you need most is an open heart, someone to talk to, and a willingness to write your true self onto the fabric of the world around you, concerning yourself less with other people's judgments and more with the common good. There's a bonus: the journey to let go of unnecessary fear can help make us into better activists—and more joyful ones too.

Fear can be debilitating. The path toward overcoming it can be thrilling. It unfolds, one mind-expanding, heart-opening, body-invigorating, community-inducing, love-soaked step at a time.

And the first step is to risk imagining something simple: the story you've lived in until today may not be the one you're doomed to stay in tomorrow.

introduction

I GREW UP AFRAID.

Fear was not unreasonable given that I had been born into a society tearing itself apart. Thousands of people were killed, tens of thousands injured, and hundreds of thousands traumatized in northern Ireland* because of their perceived political identity. My family, like many, experienced the violence directly; like many, we were equally scared of losing each other and not being able to protect ourselves. I was protected to some degree by the privilege of living in a "safer" neighborhood, but we were still vulnerable, and no one was fully exempt from the Troubles. As a teenager, I compensated by joining a religious community that was a strange and wonderful mix: life-giving (we believed that every human being is invited to a beautiful life of service and sharing), progressive (we cared about poverty and wanted to build bridges between Protestants and Catholics),

---

* I spell the name of my homeland with a lowercase *n* because of the divisions among our people over what to call it. People who identify as Irish tend to call it "the North" or "the Six Counties"; people who identify as British tend to call it "Northern Ireland." I claim mixed heritage—Catholic, Protestant, Irish, British—and think of it as belonging to everyone and no one. Changing the spelling is one part of attempting to change the story.

confused (our god threatened to torture us forever if we didn't believe the right doctrines but loved us so much that he* would grow us an extra limb if we needed one), and morally puritanical (in matters of sex but not money).

I grew up afraid in my house, and my anxiety could be triggered by anything, including the weather, the television, and the date. I grew up afraid of my country, where bomb scares were a fact of life and where ethnic enmities mean that to even *call* it a country is contentious. I grew up afraid of my body, which didn't know how to accept itself and was dehumanized by puritanical religion every time it tried. And I grew up afraid of God—who, I was told, loved me just as I was but was still determined to make me into something else.

I grew up afraid, and it took me until my midthirties to conceive that there were other ways to live—that happiness is possible, even when you've experienced so much shaming at the hands of a religious and political culture that even *you* become convinced that you deserve the hatred. Even when you've considered stopping your own heart because the pain of your stories seemed too great. Even when you've hurt others because you lacked the wisdom, maturity, and grace to recognize the impact of your actions on them. Even when you feel like the minimal conditions for hope have been swept away by a tsunami of guilt, grief, and fear. Even when you have become so overwhelmed by terror that it really might deserve to be called *possession.*

And then . . . something new. Well, actually, it's something old. Perhaps let's just say something unexpected.

Fear became a portal. A doorway to a more exciting, peaceful, useful, *whole* life. It came, like Yeats wrote of peace, "dropping slow." And the funny thing was that moving *beyond* fear seemed to depend on knowing what it's like to be *overcome*

---

*   This god isn't enlightened enough to accept a gender-neutral pronoun.

by it. You can't know what it's like to feel unafraid unless you know the intimacies of terror. You can't really experience joy unless you've known sorrow; confidence feels more real to those touched by anxiety; the beauty of the skyline is more immediately remarkable when you're wading through an ugly swamp. I heard a lot of stories of terror when I was a child, but I also remember gorgeous mountains and holy wells and steak and kidney pies and Live Aid. Far more important than that, I tasted friendship: with people, with the earth, with something Good, beyond and near at the same time.

Now—sometimes, at least—fear enlivens me. Sometimes terror turns into excitement. This book is about lessons I learned—and am learning still—on that journey, offered in hopes that they might help you too. Because in the deepest sense, what has happened to me has also happened to you. Of course there are greater and lesser wounds, injustices, and fears. Of course some suffer in ways most of us can only imagine. Of course much of the suffering in the world derives from other people's choices, ranging from the bully in a playground or parliament to political, economic, and cultural systems. None of us can truly *know* the fear of another.

Yet as you navigate whatever fear snaps at your heels or has you in its grip, you're not as alone as you may think. Whether your fear is about shame, illness, money, relationships, depression, power, prejudice, meaning, or the collapse of civilization itself, I promise you that if we stick to the path together, we'll be OK.

I began writing this book as I was emerging from being cloaked in fear, and it has evolved since then over more than a decade of stumbling, setbacks, and the continuous grace of learning. Looking back, I think that growing up afraid has become an asset, and I am genuinely grateful for my journey to the edge. I'm grateful for the fear and the nearness to death that I have felt because they teach me that I am alive. They direct me to notice the miraculous every day. I don't always live in this place, but I am learning to visit more often.* There are times when I choose to believe that the bare trees in front of my office window have shed dead leaves at least partly so that I can see the mountains behind them, that the breaking of my heart and the bending of my mind are not really what I thought they were. They are better understood as the breaking of a hard shell that contained my heart and an opening of my mind to begin to transcend the fear of sharing my gifts. The experience of four decades of not dying insists that no matter how difficult circumstances may seem, today is not my forever. Fear is not a life sentence but a gift. Part of the gift only lives when it's shared.

So here goes.

THERE'S AN EDGY but delicate movie called *Heist* (2001) about the kind of thieves who distinguish themselves by rhetorical eloquence and wry one-liners. In response to the assertion that he's a "pretty smart fella," the master burglar, played by Gene Hackman, offers the following: "I'm not that smart. I tried to imagine a fella smarter than myself. Then I tried to think, *What would he do?*"

Rogues are often capable of ageless insight. Before you can become wise, you need to admit that you're not.

There are three typical responses to fear: fight, flee, or freeze. These three responses are really stories we tell ourselves about what to do with fear. When we are afraid, we repeat stories we have learned that say we must either lash out, run away, or be immobilized. Sometimes, because of the stories we tell in our fear, we hurt others: we lash out at family members or start

----

* Thanks to my friend Nance Pettit for this beautiful way of thinking about spiritual growth.

wars. Sometimes, in our fear, we try to escape from the voices in our heads, and we leave unfinished the work we are here to do and the gifts we are here to share. Sometimes, in our fear, we go numb, stay stuck, and do nothing. We miss life, and the people we could share it with miss *us*. Fighting back against fear tends to provoke a rebound of even more aggressive, fearful reaction; running away from it diminishes our lives; freezing changes nothing.

These three stories we tell in response to fear are totally natural, and while they may carry us through immediate danger, they don't help us grow. I have spent most of my life overwhelmed by fear. The three stories dominated my thoughts and actions: fight, flee, freeze, and repeat. They took me to the edge. Terrors colonized my imagination. I became desperate.

I'm not that smart. So like Gene Hackman's character, I tried to imagine what someone smarter than me would do. Over time, I discovered a bit of wisdom that changed everything.

There is a fourth story.

This book is called *How Not to Be Afraid*, but it's not about eliminating fear. It's about learning how to feel fear without being driven by it. It's about knowing the difference between healthy fear and paranoia. It's about becoming tender enough with ourselves and connecting enough with our true selves to find the gift *underneath* the fear.

Fear doesn't go away—nor should it. At times it helps us make wise decisions: put on your seat belt, don't put your hand in that tiger's cage, slow down. And at times, our fear is about loss—the sickness or death of a loved one, for instance—and must be held with great tenderness. The problem is when fear becomes the lens through which we see everything. We're often afraid of the wrong things, or we fear the right things the wrong way. Then we find it difficult or impossible to tell the difference between the story in our head and what we're actually facing.

The first thing you notice when you experience fear as much as I have is that you don't want to. It's unpleasant. It gets in the way. It often feels like a waste of time, and at the same time, it feels impossible to do anything about it.

A wise friend once told me that 90 percent of our fears do not reflect reality at all. I have spent years searching for the peer-reviewed psychology journal article in which that statistic is published. I haven't found it yet, but it has more than a ring of truth. How many times have I faced something that seemed terrifying but then wasn't as bad as I had feared? And even more often, the thing I was afraid of simply didn't happen at all. Fear and danger are not the same thing. We tend to overstate the presence of danger, imagining peril where there is none, and we often underappreciate what we can do about the threats that actually exist. If we don't learn what to do with fear, we may miss the beauty of each ordinary day lived in community, in service to the common good,* in gratitude for the astonishing gift of simply being alive.

There's an old idea that the fear of God is the beginning of wisdom. I'm going to risk suggesting that this idea has been fundamentally misunderstood. It doesn't mean that there's a Scary Bearded Guy in the sky who loves you so much that he will kill you if you don't agree with him. It means that becoming wise begins with honoring reality. There is a healthy way to be afraid that helps us live better and an unhealthy one that makes us sick. There is a well-worn but sometimes hidden path that can help us discern the difference.

Traveling along this path won't show us how not to fear at all, but it can help us figure out *how* to be—and how *not* to be—afraid. The path is not difficult—in fact, in some respects,

---

* The common good is not just about humans but the entire ecosystem. Of course, humans are part of the ecosystem too. What is truly good for the ecosystem and what is truly good for humans cannot be unraveled.

it is much easier than the alternative of being overwhelmed by fear. What might be difficult is trusting that there is a different way of being and then practicing it.

We're going to explore some aspects of this path in the coming pages. But before we do that, I want to welcome you properly. I imagine you're here because you know fear well, either in yourself or in a loved one. You are looking for some comfort, some connection, some ideas that might help. Thank you for coming. I'm glad we're here together. As I write, I'm thinking about you with tenderness and respect. I'm wondering about the journey that has brought you here, what keeps you awake or goes bump in your night. I'm imagining that you may have despaired of ever being free of the terror you experience, or the shame you feel, or the sense that you're a burden to others. You are not alone, and you are so welcome here. It's my job to show you that what I just said is true.

Fear is a natural response to the world as we see it. At times it is an inevitable biological reaction. At times it is necessary to keep us safe. I'd be more worried about you if you never felt fear. But our fears are also reactions to the story we believe. The authority to tell a story may be more powerful than the ability to launch missiles, and these days we live in a world of overactive competition to tell the story. Old certainties—some healthy, some not—are under serious question. New platforms, opportunities, and invitations for telling stories are emerging. Never before have we had more public storytelling and fewer agreed-upon gatekeepers to help us decide what is wise, what is factual, what is a matter of opinion or taste, and what is pure propaganda or conspiracy. While it is sometimes obvious, it is not always easy to discern whether the storytellers we're listening to are nurturing the common good or merely their own egos, bank balances, or dominance.

We live in a time when so much seems uncertain: the stability of the climate; the relationships within and between nations;

confidence about public health and economic security; the possibility of overcoming racism with beloved community; whether or not we will ever again feel safe from violence, authoritarianism, or pandemics. Things that previous generations seemed to take for granted now seem entirely in question.

But even the people who lived in the "good old days" yearned for the "good old days." Every generation makes up a story about a happier past and wishes for a better future. Unless we learn wisdom, the present rarely makes sense until it's over. So even though we might see the past through rose-colored glasses, it's no wonder so many of us feel anxious. It is difficult to sort through the noise to find reliable sources of comfort. If trauma is what happens when a profound wound is not met with adequate empathy, it's no wonder so many of us in this moment feel traumatized: the ground has shifted beneath our feet, and few of the structures and voices we relied on have proven able to reassure us.

A few years ago, having reached the point of apparent helplessness in the face of obsessive fear—about violence, homophobia, my place in the world, and my fantasy of God's judgment of me—I took a clinical questionnaire to self-assess for the symptoms of post-traumatic stress disorder (PTSD). The questionnaire ended with the assertion that a yes response to more than two questions might indicate the presence of PTSD. Out of forty questions, I had answered yes to thirty-eight.

Aside from this being one of the few times I ever got better than a B on a test, I felt relieved. I was not crazy after all. Having lived with the symptoms of PTSD for decades, I was soon properly diagnosed. I found that the attention of a good therapist, trained in tending to such woundedness, can radically transform one's experience of the world.

Dave the Therapist told me he didn't like the word *disorder*. He preferred to call it post-traumatic *stuff*, because there's nothing disordered about reacting fearfully to abnormal circumstances. Such reactions are totally normal; it's the *circumstances* that are disordered. We'll get to more of this later, but in this moment, if you are experiencing things that seem like the symptoms of post-traumatic *stuff* or other anxiety *stuff* or just feeling a little nervous about continuing, I invite you right now to pause your reading and go to the section at the end of chapter 1 called "An Invitation to Take a Breath." Come back here when you feel ready. There's no hurry. (You can, of course, also skip to this section any time while reading the book.)

How Not to Be Afraid is not a replacement for therapy or medication thoughtfully prescribed, but I hope that reading it alongside good therapy will help. Writing it that way has certainly helped me. It's also worth noting that the root words for what we understand as "therapy"—*therapeia theôn*—carried the sense of "caring for the gods." Part of the therapy we may all need, and are all called to offer, is to tend to the voices within and help them find their rightful place in the drama and comedy of life. The stories we tell are, in a certain sense, gods. How we receive and work with or challenge them will help determine their power over us. It may be the gods at the present moment who need more help than us.

Perhaps the voices inside you—the terrifying stories that interrupt and threaten to capsize you—are themselves gods asking for your help, or maybe just your attention. Just as it can be difficult to tell the difference between depression and discernment, one of the first tasks we face in fear is to decide what truth the fear is trying to tell us about our cosmic selves and our small world. Then we can decide what to do with it.

With that in mind, this book won't teach you how not to *feel* fear, but it might help you find better ways to *work with* fear. It could perhaps just as easily be titled *How to Be Afraid Well.* It is intended to help you feel less alone and show you some steps you can take to transform your fears into better stories about who you truly are. I'm willing to bet that who you truly are is much more valuable than you think.

<hr style="width:30%">

FEAR IS ONE of the most powerful things we cannot see—universally recognized and with implications for everything in life: relationships, health, politics, and even the limits of what we can hope for as a species. Yet there is something more powerful than fear, and it is also available to everyone, all the time. That "something" is the *stories we tell.*

How Not to Be Afraid is based on the idea that popular beliefs about fear are mistaken and that we can transform our fear through storytelling. Love—the willingness to give ourselves for the sake of the common good—is the foundation from which these better stories emerge, becoming the antidote to fear. A small, bad idea cannot be erased. Yet it can be replaced by a larger and better story.

So here's a larger, better story that you might wish to try on. Fighting, fleeing, and freezing are all natural reactions to fear and sometimes may be the least bad options we can see. However, they are all manifestations of oppositional, not creative, energy—and just as we know war is not a solution to the world's problems, "battling" fear does not work either. What does work is learning the path of a better story, lived in community, grounded by elders, and with a purpose beyond personal gain. Without the kind of creative empathy that emerges in such a story, we may blame ourselves for more errors than we could possibly have committed. We may fear more booby traps than could ever actually be laid. We may feel that we are responsible for fixing everything, and feeling overwhelmed will be a completely familiar experience. Finding our place in a better story can help us let go of our tendency to try to control things that should never be our burden alone. More than that, while the stories embodied in our fear are often distortions of reality, learning how not to be afraid means tenderly seeking

the wisdom underneath the raw material of our most terrorized moments.

Instead of erasing our fears by trying to beat them away or
getting "around" them, perhaps we can transcend and include
them, even in the very core of our being. This means not pretending that there is no trouble in the world or that "It's not
my problem." Indeed, the current moment* has stirred anxiety
in profound ways, and each of us has a responsibility—and a
gift—to share in helping.

Some things are indeed worthy of a healthy fear, but they
are usually not the things that distract us the most. We should
be afraid of mosquitoes more than people, of cars more than
war. Most of all, we might be wiser to fear the unlived life more
than the monster under the bed. Yet whatever we're afraid of,
we are invited not to deny our fears but to tell a bigger story
about them.

Many of us feel overwhelmed by anxiety, exhausted by activism, and at times even in dread of the future. Yet these feelings of
anxiety, exhaustion, and dread derive their power from a story.
We're here to uncover how story shapes our lives, to take a look
at how fears depend on the story we tell about them, and to imagine a new story. The story we believe about fear was probably
built by someone else, who may or may not have known wisdom
about what was best for us; that's only one of the reasons that we
don't necessarily have to believe it anymore, although we probably do need help to discover and build a new one.

It will not serve us to speak of *fighting* or seeking to *defeat*
fear, because adversarial force always boomerangs. Instead, we

---

*   When speaking of the current moment, we might mean the day you're
reading this, the past few years, the decades since the turn of the millennium, the period since World War II or the Industrial Revolution,
or even further back toward our ancient cultural foundations. Each
moment has its own anxieties, its own traumas, its own real dangers
and imagined threats—its own gifts of healing and transformation too.

are invited to be engaged in *creating* a shelter for larger, more truthful stories. Better stories about fear can transform these burdens into fuel for a more beautiful life, for a more peaceful world, helping us find calm amid the storm. When the shelter is strong, better stories can even guide and empower us to help calm the storm itself. This book is about how to build that shelter.

part 1

chapter 1

what are you afraid of?

Courage is . . . mastery of fear, not
absence of fear.

— Mark Twain

GENERATIONS SUFFERED IN northern Ireland's violence,
and like many, our family was directly affected. Some of my
loved ones lost friends, witnessed multiple bombings, or lived
with constant background nervousness about what might be
around the next corner. Most northern Irish people my generation and older experienced the suffocating effects of sectarian
enmity, and multitudes know its grief. The way we talked about
the violence—each week a litany of murder—left me accustomed
to the idea that killing was just the way things had to be. This
was, so we were told, the story of our lives. My parents protected
me from the dominance of this narrative as best they could, but
I was born into it, and I couldn't hide.

This, of course, was not the whole story. There was also
beauty and friendship all around us all the time; the terrible
things that were done in our conflict were often followed by
extraordinary acts of courage and humanity on the part of

survivors and their communities. The eventually evolving mercies of a peace process have now delivered substantial cooperation between former sworn enemies.

But the way we had learned to tell and rehearse the story—from political and cultural leaders, religion, and the media—emphasized human cruelty on one hand and human brokenness on the other. In the stories we told most loudly, there was little room for human ingenuity, for the spark of cooperation, for psychologically and spiritually integrated lament for the wound, for courageous creativity toward the common good. The shadow of fear and death, of the feelings and beliefs we repressed, became the whole projection of our lives. Light struggled to flicker. We were struggling to learn how to bind our wounds or to show just mercy to those who had caused them. Many of us did not know how to speak about our shared responsibility for creating a society in which some lives were worth more than others. It made sense that two wrongs don't make a right in ordinary daily life, but we seemed unable to extend the proverb to a centuries-old ethnic conflict. Hope was enacted by countless brave individuals who put themselves between violence and the vulnerable. Yet in public, hope was often merely a sentimental quality rationed out at Christmas and church, rarely getting to the heart of what we should actually do to embody it.

Having lived in a society marked by violent civil conflict throughout my entire childhood and having participated in a small way in a peace process that has proven the value of talking to enemies instead of killing them, I am still being transformed in midlife by learning to tell the story differently. It has been a long journey, still ongoing, for me to learn to honor real suffering while overcoming the fear that things are perpetually getting worse. And the same is true for many of us, regardless of where we came from. Our news feeds are colonized by horrific images and bullying rhetoric. Despite the prevalence of funny videos and wholesome memes—not to mention stories of hopeful transformation—many of us feel that we are living with more fear than we used to know. More than we can handle.

But things may not be as bad as they may seem. The average human is living in arguably the most peaceable time we have ever known, at least since people emerged. But that is not the story we're telling ourselves. If you looked at "the news" today—perhaps especially if you did so half asleep in bed or absentmindedly over lunch—you might have had difficulty discerning the *meaning* of the horror in Somalia or San Diego, the celebrity mishap in Beverly Hills, or the report about climate change everywhere. As stories gain electronic traction, they are treated with equal urgency, and a sane sense of proportion disappears. The same red strip announcing "Breaking News" rushes across the screen no matter whether it is actually breaking or even really news.

The spiritual implications of online culture are only beginning to be recognized, and they contain both benefits and challenges. The sudden emergence of near-universal access to exponentially increasing sources of knowledge is a magnificent thing. I have beside me an item made of glass and metal that fits in my palm and connects me instantly with a repository of nearly everything human beings know that can be written down or illustrated. It can teach me, heal me, grant me access to new relationships, and solidify old ones. It can even spark the fires of justice. It's a magic box.

Yet the emergence of a virtual public sphere that compels us to believe we should all have an opinion about everything and that we must publish that opinion before we've had the chance to truly think about it is not a magnificent thing. This item, which is the size of a deck of cards, has on it little pictures that I can press and be instantly transported into a world of infinite content, much of which is antithetical to the common good. It can waste my time, trigger my anger, tempt me to gossip, encourage me to trample on other people's vulnerability, and trick me into thinking that everything is my business. It can bombard me with enough anxiety stimulation to keep me afraid, some-where inside, all the time. This machine gives—or even compels—immediate, unfiltered access to a veritable fear industry, and on the path it forges lies the fracturing of our relationships with ourselves, with our neighbors, and with the earth itself.

Terrible things have always happened; they happen today, and they will happen tomorrow. But these stories are often told either by voices or in environments that may seem authoritative but offer neither a context that explains them accurately nor wis-dom about how to transform conflict. There are, of course, many honorable journalists, and the internet has vastly diversified the voices with access to being published. It's easier than ever to get behind the headlines, to discover a more complex story in which boundless hope and proportionate lament exist alongside finite trouble. That complex story is also more truthful, and there's a chance we humans may evolve into widely embracing it.

But for now, at least, we have to consciously choose to look for it. Many of the loudest voices still divide the world into "us" and "them," still suggest that security will come from "us" beating "them," and still present reality as if it were a series of booby traps. So it's no wonder that many of us feel that we are living in the midst of an expanding epidemic of violence. This is partly because the way we tell stories mirrors the way the reactive part of our brains experiences them: triggered by spectacles and unable to easily absorb gradual change toward peace or an absence of violence.

It is also partly a result of increased empathy, as the circle of who the dominant We include in our definition of Us is expanding. The cultures from which some of us are descended used to send children up chimneys or down mine shafts and executed people in public, sometimes as a form of entertainment. Women and people of color were denied the vote, and some people were criminalized for being in love. Today the incidence of child labor has been de-creasing, the use of the death penalty has decreased worldwide, the expansion of civil rights continues in law and culture alike, and the lives of LGBTQ+ people are more visible and more respected. While still we rise, there are more and more life stories considered worthy of respect, of a place at the table.

So when pain is visible in the faces of folks around the world or across town—people who in the past were either held at arm's length or dehumanized by people who held power in top-down societies—today those of us used to privilege may be more likely to feel some of that pain within ourselves. Despite those stories of terror and pain, it seems humans generally are actually experiencing less violence over time, and the possibilities of further peaceableness may be even better.

This is not to deny the existence of violence, prejudice, and inequality or to downplay the real trouble in our world. But even if there were no evidence of reduced violence, there is still reason for hope. It is true that each killing, each act of hate, each involuntary separation is a universe to the victim's loved ones. Solidarity with the suffering of others is both a part of the privilege of being human and a step toward a future in which no one will have to suffer that way again. And such solidarity seems to be growing.

It is important not to deny these truths: that by many measures, the world is getting better and that expanding circles of sympathy mean that more lives are considered worthy. It is also important to recognize that despite the reduction in violence and poverty and advances in health and communication, many of us don't feel good much of the time. Though we may not be living through an epidemic of increasing violence, we do seem to be experiencing an epidemic of *fear.*

The most insidious of fear's powers is the ability to lead people to act violently toward themselves and others. Most of us have not physically harmed someone else, but we may have denied the fullness of another, withheld compassion from someone, or prevented our own flourishing because we have not been introduced to an alternative to the fear story. If you want to create chaos, teach people to be afraid. If you want to increase violence, give in to your fear. But if you want to reduce violence, you can adopt practices that not only will make you less afraid but could actually help everyone you meet to do the same.

These practices will help you live in a story that is both more true and more hopeful. That's what we're here to do: to uncover how stories shape our lives, to take a look at how fears depend on the story we tell about them, and to learn to imagine a new story. This new story might help reorient your mind, your habits, your relationships, and your sense of self. Fear then becomes not a destination on the other side of a sign that reads "Abandon Hope" but an invitation to a life full of excitement, meaning, and love.

CATERING TO FEAR and pessimism is a function of the most dangerous belief: that violence can bring order out of chaos. Healing the world requires recognizing the damage that this story has done. While we lament real wounds and work to prevent them, we acknowledge that it was the stories we told that got us into trouble in the first place. If some things are getting better, we can learn why, and we can make them better still. This is as true for the creative arts of television and cinema, literature, games, and music as for their nonfiction counterparts.

The real news about your world does not begin with the flashing red strip across the bottom of the screen. It begins even before you engage any media or form of craft; *it begins in your mind*, with the story you're telling about yourself. It interacts with those stories told by your loved ones and neighbors to create a bigger story. It connects with every place you go—on foot or by chair or online.

This story is much more important than the news. It is the single most important element in determining our happiness and the kind of life we will lead. It is immensely powerful, though most of us aren't conscious of this, much of the time. The story we tell ourselves influences our perceptions of physical threat and both the antagonism and the blessing we direct toward ourselves. And even if the world does become more dangerous, the story you tell yourself will determine the part you play: as either a courageous, wounded healer (of yourself and others) or merely a victim of other people's broken stories.

We all struggle with some form of fear, but few of us seem to experience the struggle as a gift. The emotion we call fear is only energy passing through us. It can, like electrical circuitry, empower, but if it is not contained in a system that will safely direct its flow, it can kill. Some fear is healthy and true, and some fear is unhealthy and false. When we feel afraid, it can be useful to ponder the fear beneath the fear. What is it that I am *really* afraid of? Am I really afraid of losing my reputation, or of cancer, or of violence, or of the collapse of civilization as we know it? Usually the fear *beneath* the fear matters more than what's on the surface. Frequently, what I'm actually afraid of is not being able to cope if any of those things were to happen.

But people *have* coped—even thrived—after losing their reputation, while suffering a terminal illness, in the aftermath of violence, and even when the world around them collapsed. The people who have lived well through such apparent disasters are the ones who own their stories rather than being ruled by someone else's.

In this book, we'll explore seven common fears and look at seven ways to live better while facing them. The power our fears have over us depends on the stories we tell about them. And while our stories are enormously diverse, there are a few fears we may all have in common. These are the seven fears we'll explore together:

1. Fear of being alone
2. Fear of having done something that can't be fixed
3. Fear of a meaningless life
4. Fear of not having enough

5. Fear that you'll be broken forever
6. Fear of the world
7. Fear of death

The first part of this book takes a look at what fear is, why we are afraid, and the central idea of building a shelter in which a better story can grow. Part 2, then, is devoted to the seven fears, sharing stories about how they manifest and offering a way to move through them. All these fears overlap, so our exploration will do that also. You might learn something about the fear of not having enough while reading about the fear of being alone, for instance.

At the end of each chapter in part 1 is an invitation: a chance to do something that opens your mind and heart to the idea of fear as a contorted story and that lays the foundations of a better one. The seven chapters in part 2 each conclude with a practice to help you step into a way of living better and transform your fear. These are the seven ways to live better promised by the book's subtitle. All the invitations and ways can and should be used at any time you feel you need them. But as they speak to different parts of our lives, if you step into them one at a time, a significant transformation might await.

The invitations and practices are rooted in what has become known as the *contemplative tradition*, in which saints facing great difficulty—personal loss, plagues, war—discovered and evolved practices to help them not run away from the world but *face* it. Contemplative practices like meditation are not merely intended to help us feel better; they are capable of producing humans who know what we're here for—to love and be loved—and who then do it, no matter how scary things seem.

If you recognize yourself in any of those seven fears, you might receive your first comfort: *none of us is alone in our fear.* Whatever has terrorized you may also have terrorized me. It has almost certainly terrorized someone you know and love. But the power of that terror depends on the story we tell about it. Let's reimagine that story.

AN INVITATION TO TAKE A BREATH

WE COME NOW to the first invitation. Each of the invitations in this book is about replacing an unhelpful ritual with a life-giving one. Practicing them regularly, even when you don't feel the need, will build spiritual "muscle memory," making it easier to live from the brilliant, beautiful, resilient, dangerous, creative true self we are here to discover.

Gaining some more control over the pace of our breathing may be the most effective step we can take toward transforming fear. It will also help us on our path toward finding a better story with a better center, and the ego might even calm down a bit too. Neuroscience tells us that how we breathe affects how we think, and more recent research and practice in what is called *sensorimotor psychotherapy* go even further: how you walk affects how you feel. Consider slowing the pace at which you move by just a little bit, and notice how your thoughts begin to change. Slow down. It will speed up your ability to heal.

I'm doing it now. Would you like to join me? First, find a quiet place to sit, one in which there are few other distractions, and breathe. Allow your breathing to slow down to a rhythm that is long but unforced. Take long, luxurious breaths in and out, noticing and even enjoying the rising and falling of your chest. Don't hold your breath; just let it lengthen.

With your eyes open, call to mind something that sparks a smile or gratitude or love. It could be the face of a loved one, or a life-giving quotation from your favorite writer, or a place you love to visit, or even part of a favorite movie or book. Breathe slowly—not forcing it, just gently. Breathe.

Let the image get bigger and clearer as you breathe. (When I do this exercise, I like to picture the image projected onto an enormous outdoor movie screen in front of a mountain. It looks pretty spectacular that way.) As the image or thought gets clearer, keep breathing.

Do this for a minute or longer. Don't pay attention to distractions, and don't judge yourself for being distracted. Just keep breathing.

When the image is really clear, take one big breath in.

And then exhale, and while doing so, with your mind, send the image to every cell of your body.

Then do it again. Breathe in. Feel yourself inhaling the smile, the gratitude, or the love. Hold your breath for a second or two.

And then exhale, sending the image to every cell of your body.

You can pause there if you like, but you can also take it further. Breathe in, but this time when you breathe out, send the image to people you know who might need it: people in your community, your city, the nation, the world.

You can respond to this invitation any time you like. Don't do it while driving or operating heavy machinery (except when the heavy machinery is your mind). Also, if you experience something like the symptoms of PTSD or an anxiety disorder as you try this, know that you are not alone. Ask someone for help. Treatment with a wise person who understands the range of therapeutic support can make a huge difference.

This exercise can be done in a minute or so, or you can spend hours on it. With a wee bit of practice, you can do it anywhere, all the time, every breath you take.

chapter 2

fear is a story

Fear is an incompetent teacher.

—Jean-Luc Picard

MY CHILDHOOD WAS overshadowed by the threat of violence and sectarian division, challenging my capacity to feel safe or to find a place to belong. The paradox of being human—made for love and service but taught to dominate and compete—is made far more obvious in a divided society.

We could argue all day about who started the conflict in and about northern Ireland, who suffered the most, and who is most responsible, but that's not our purpose here. In this context, what matters most to me is that some of us experienced suffering as a result of choices made on all sides, and while it's often convenient to identify with one or the other party in a political conflict, we all contain multitudes. This is true wherever we may live, whatever our particular political conflicts may be. And although no two places are the same, perhaps exploring the specifics of northern Ireland—or at least the story I have come to tell about it—might illuminate whatever conflicts and fears may be arising where you are.

My birth family is both northern Irish and southern Irish, both English and Scottish, both Protestant and Catholic. My great-grandmother on my mother's side was a Russian Jew who fled anti-Semitic violence in the land of her birth. For me to even be here, between world wars, pogroms, and civil conflicts, at least five people escaped getting killed. My lineage is Protestant, it is Catholic, it is Jewish, and it is of those whose loves I do not know. And yet I've been told that there are only two kinds of people in my home society: unionists or nationalists, Protestants or Catholics, and some less polite terminology too. This complicates things. Being human is a paradox. And so is the search for peace. How can I be reconciled with the "other side" when I don't know what side I'm from? What does the other side look like? Whose side is it anyway? Is it possible that what we hold dear and wish to protect—in other words, what lies behind our fear—is just a story? And if it's just a story, can it be rewritten?

WHEN I WAS growing up, we didn't know who to trust. The conflict—and the stories we told about it—dominated our lives. Simple, everyday actions like opening doors, turning car-ignition keys, going to the movies, getting a taxi, or having a conversation with a stranger became fraught with suspicion. Would there be someone lurking behind the door? Would the cinema be evacuated because of a bomb under a car outside? Would the stranger be one of those lovely friends you hadn't met yet, or would they tell other strangers things about you that could get you killed? Was your loved one dead or just stuck in traffic?

No matter what side of the community we lived on, many of us knew that thousands of our neighbors sharing the same land might have seemed satisfied to see us suffer. Things were often tense, with arguments precipitated by some new atrocity, a family member losing a loved one or a friend finding a hoax bomb in a warehouse while hundreds of people shopped a few feet away. These stories of personal terror were well hidden when I was a child because my parents wanted to protect me from the trauma of living in a political nightmare. I didn't realize until later that my mixed background made me not fit in anywhere. In a society that consistently normalized the abnormal, where things children should never witness became nothing more than politics as usual, where your opinion about an invisible land border could get you killed, I knew I did not belong. Not Protestant enough to be seen as fully British, not Catholic enough to be seen as fully Irish, I was discontentedly confused with my demographic lot.

This was the story we told: That you must support either northern Ireland remaining in the United Kingdom or the political reunification of Ireland. That whoever the "other side" was had caused the conflict in the first place and that "our" side was merely defending itself. That we were living in a nice place that was also a bit like hell and nobody knew how to fix it. That "we" were right and "they" were wrong. That if only we could defeat our enemies, we could enjoy the spectacular natural beauty of our landscape, the exquisite imaginations of our poets and artists, the warm hospitality for which we were reputed by tourist guides. The problem for me is that I couldn't be sure who my "we" was.

But amid the horror of the violence used on behalf of all sides of our divided community (though with very little active consent), there was another story underway. Quiet, immense strength was manifesting among people willing to forgo divisive ideology in favor of the common good. Many people were willing to let go of the old certainties about winning and create communities of beautiful, life-giving ambiguity rather than the superficial gratification of being "right." People were allowing their imaginations to be funded by the heart, the mind, and experimentation rather than dogma. People were refusing to use violence to get what they wanted and were caring for the suffering and the bereaved. People were initiating conversations with their political opponents, including those who might harm them, and moving into neighborhoods where they didn't "belong" in order to show that *everyone* belongs. People were laying aside vengeance in favor of cooperation.

Until I was nineteen years old, active civil conflict continued in northern Ireland. Through painstaking work, courage, and forbearance, since then, we have still been learning how to talk with each other instead, although we sometimes still face the violence that some people believe will advance their cause. Many of us look back on our history of violent conflict with a mix of grief, regret, and shame. We may still want to be right, but we're learning that it's better to be creative.

My personal pain is less than many and greater than some, but there are few consolations to competitive suffering. What unites many survivors of violence, no matter the particular shape of our wounds, is the desire to prevent what happened to us from happening to others. What is uniting some of us even more is the notion that weaving a pathway through suffering must coexist with giving ourselves to the conscious experience of beauty. Even as we witness the wounds of violence and work to repair and prevent them, we will be well served by noticing the rainbows in the distance, the aroma of fresh-cut grass, the butterflies by the side of the road.*

Yet appreciating the butterflies does not make us naive. We know from experience that turning our fear and rage onto others is not a recipe for anybody's well-being. Some of us recognize that a willingness to die to protect the vulnerable should be valued more highly than a willingness to kill. We are coming to believe that peace is the way to itself and that every story we tell can help heal us or kill us. We are all called to be peaceful warrior-protectors for the common good.

It has been said that the antidote to fear is not optimism but action rooted in hope. Such hope comes from each of us taking the steps that we can, coming together in community, bringing

---

*   For a specific and moving historical example of an Irish person noticing butterflies by the side of the road amid painful circumstances and many other examples of beauty coexisting with struggle, see Rebecca Solnit's passionate book *Hope in the Dark.*

our gifts, and asking for what we need. If our stories tell us we are doomed, or if our stories blame others alone for our predicament, or if our stories separate people into "us" and "them," it shouldn't be surprising that we lack hope. But if we cut into the shell of a corroded story and allow some light in, something really wonderful happens: our experience changes.

I live in the United States now, which grants me the opportunity to compare the strife of my youth and the peace process of my early adult life with the political climate in another beautiful and broken place. A recent political interview revealed a truth by accident when a national figure well-known for stirring up public discord responded to a journalist's evidence-based affirmation that violence had actually been reducing for decades. "Theoretically [you] may be right," the politician said, "but it's not where human beings are. . . . As a political candidate, I'll go with how people feel, and I'll let you go with the theoreticians." Even if that's what he really believes, how sad. He may not know it, but he's replicating a well-worn myth, one that keeps human beings afraid and controlled. He and his colleagues could help lead people out of this prison, but he's trapped in it too.

MAYBE THIS HYPOTHESIS can help: the stories we tell shape how we experience everything. When we tell a diminished story, we make a diminished life. The culture many of us have been born into embodies both stories that diminish and stories that elevate. They're in a dance with each other, but one side often seems to have the volume turned much higher.

Here are some of the dominant, diminishing stories our culture often recites, apparently without asking if they are true.

We are born into darkness. Emerging from it will require fighting our way out of it, even if that means hurting or killing other people.

Winning is everything. Get as much as you can, keep as much as
     you can, and give some away for the sake of your conscience.
The past is a list of honorable military victories. In these con-
     flicts, the methods "we" used were always righteous, but the
     actions of our opponents never were.
There's nothing most of us can do to change things. Your job is
     to consume things that other people have made and not to
     worry too much about how they made it.
People engaged in peacemaking are naive and unrealistic. Or,
     possibly, they are so heroic and unusual that their actions
     can't be emulated. The expression of anger is antithetical
     to peacemaking.
Religion and politics are about moral purity, community bound-
     aries, and being right. Our society is organized to keep us
     much of the time disconnected in vehicles and "safe" behind
     walls.
This is one of the most violent times in history to be alive. This
     is just the way things are, but despite the chaos of the world,
     we have violence on our side too, because violence brings
     order out of chaos and can literally redeem things.

These stories are widely believed, but they are not true. In
his poem "The Skylight," Seamus Heaney illustrates the notion
that sometimes the most valuable gifts come from allowing another perspective to tell a new story. He begins by resisting his
wife's wish for a skylight in their house. He preferred their roof
the way it was: snug. A skylight would destroy the comfort of a
contained space. But when the roof is cut open and the skylight
placed, Heaney is transformed. So profound is the change that he
reaches for a miraculous analogy: he is bathed in "extravagant
sky," now feeling as if he had witnessed healing from paralysis.
The skylight he had opposed—the thing he believed could only
diminish his life—turned out to contain the very *seeds* of life. It
opened him to a new story, and nothing was ever the same.

Something like this can happen here too. Such miracles await anyone willing to cut into the boundaries of the story they've been telling themselves. Better stories can let the light in.

We tell stories of separation, selfishness, and scapegoating so well that they are often an unquestioned default reaction to our circumstances. How many movies have you seen in which the hero "solves" the matter merely by shooting / blowing up / crushing the villain? Then again, how many movies have you seen that offer creative and less lethal solutions, or tell the stories of nonviolent transformation, or meaningfully trace why villains become villains in the first place? Meanwhile, how many national political movements embody genuine cooperation across lines of difference? Might there be a relationship between the amount of energy we give to stories in which a destructive force wipes out, neutralizes, or aggressively humiliates its opponents before walking away, literally cleansing the world, and the winner-takes-all mentality that gives rise to social conflict, authoritarian politics, and many wars? And might there be a relationship between that way of telling the story of the world and how frightened so many of us feel every day?

Stories of connection, courage, creativity, and the common good are more true but less frequently told. Given that the brain more easily recalls shocks than wisdom and notices spectacles more easily than gradual change, these better stories need to be spoken more often with more imagination. That doesn't always mean they need to be longer. *Love your neighbor as yourself* is a very short story indeed, but it may contain the secret of how all life can experience its own abundance.

But because wiser stories are often ignored, rejected, suppressed, or (most often) not told in the first place, let's consciously commit to giving more oxygen in our thinking and talking to stories like these:

In the beloved community, fear is overcome, wounds are healed, the suffering are cared for, and even the former oppressors can find a home. While many of the foundational stories told in Western culture are rooted in the notion that we define ourselves and resolve conflicts through scapegoating the other, they do not bring more peace and security. When we take steps to bring about something beyond our own personal gain, we become activists; when our actions nonviolently subvert the lies told in many of our foundational narratives, we are story activists. Here are just a handful of story activists from Turtle Island alone: the abolitionist and women's rights leader Sojourner Truth; the journalist and social activist Dorothy Day; Martin Luther King Jr.; the labor activist Dolores Huerta; the singer, actor, and civil rights activist Harry Belafonte; the theologian and violence reduction activist Walter Wink; the environmentalist and economist Winona LaDuke; and even the creator of the Muppets, Jim Henson, whose anarchic circus takes kindness as seriously as some people take war. These and millions of others, both individuals and movements, both famous and quiet, illuminate the path. Being fierce for creativity, not domination, in culture, religion, education, politics, and art is hard work and takes courage, but it also leads to some of the deepest joy a human can know.

We need to know where we have come from. Listening to the voices of Indigenous people (if we are not ourselves Indigenous) and speaking our truth (if we are) are vital. Without the practice of initiation into mature adulthood, the bearing of each other's burdens, and the respect for the circle of life, our lives are profoundly incomplete, and we may never know what to do with our fear.

Spirituality is our living relationship with mystery. There is a creative and a destructive side to religion, and at its best, religion knows how to lament wounds, educate for life, celebrate the good, and inspire change. It can help us nurture communities in which we discover how to live from the inside out rather than for external reward, in which we encourage each other to more whole lives, and from which we can serve not sectarian or party interest but the common good.

Talking with our opponents is less lethal and more effective at establishing peaceable arrangements than the use of force. This is as true for nations at war as it is for individuals who don't agree with each other. And somebody always has to go first.

Violence does not redeem anything. In fact, it creates further destabilization and long-term need. Two wrongs have never made a right, and the just war theory has more often been used as an excuse rather than actually practiced.

Most of us are living in a more peaceable world than ever. There is still violence, of course, and some places and people are suffering terribly. Yet violence appears to have generally reduced. Even in the places where it has not, and even if there are reversals, we know more than we have ever known about how to reduce it further, repair the wounds it causes, and prevent it.

Our cultural myopia makes us afraid of possible dangers lurking everywhere. But the expanding circle of empathy sensitizes us to pain we might otherwise ignore and in which we may actually have been complicit.

Rates of violence are likely linked to social inequality, racial oppression, and lack of community bonds. Nonviolent revolutions and peace processes alike have created more whole societies and resolved various conflicts by bringing enemies to the table, addressing legitimate needs, sharing power, and making amends for past injustices.

Bombing instead of talking to our enemies is the worst strategy for making peace. Even if the violence in which we're engaged is limited to character assassination, it's one end of a continuum that concludes in mutually assured destruction.

The best criticism of the bad is the practice of the better. Showering the people we hate with love is not just a nice bit of poetry; it's one of the things that will save humanity, and neither "liberals" nor "conservatives" need to violate their consciences to do it. People responsible for violence and other violations can be held to account in a way that restores dignity to survivors without dehumanizing those responsible or perpetuating a cycle of destruction. Public safety and legal remedies can be based on restorative justice principles and be good for everyone.

If it is true that the best way to transform that which mitigates against the common good is to live the change we want to see, there are profound implications for all life. Underneath violence, shame, and disconnection is fear about what we might lose or feel we have already lost. But there's something underneath that fear.

Love.

Look beneath your fear, and you will discover what it is you really care about. What you wish to protect: people, places, things, hopes, dreams. Aggression, shame, and disconnection—even as attempts at making a better life for me or a better world for all of us—don't work. But as we expand our circle of caring to include *all* people, *all* places, *all* of creation, we discover that all our fears are shared and that all our cares come from the same place. Come to understand your fear, and you may find that we're all just trying to figure out how to love. Part of that task includes learning how to hold boundaries without violence, humiliation, or self-righteousness. More than that, if the best criticism of the bad is the practice of the better, we don't have to devote as much attention to what's broken, what's ugly, what we're afraid of. We're invited to do something less broken and more beautiful instead.

THE ARTIST LAURIE Anderson paid tribute to her husband, Lou Reed, shortly after his death by outlining the shared rules for living that they had discerned together: *Don't be afraid of anyone. Get a really good bullshit detector and learn how to use it. Be really, really tender.*

These rules constitute a trinity of invitations to a space in which we take life seriously but don't take ourselves too seriously. They could serve us well, especially in a space and time where the loudest voices seem to identify more with division, despair, destruction, or defeating the other. These rules might emerge from one final wisdom story: We fear being affected by forces we cannot control, by what people think of us or what they might do to us. But we vastly underestimate our capacity to *have an impact*, to cocreate a better world.

There is a part of each of us *that cannot be impacted* by fear or pain. We usually call it the *soul* or the *true self.* I sometimes think of it as the *core beneath the core.* Many people who have suffered the most awful violation and fear also come to know that while our hearts may feel the ache of the world, our deeper selves are somehow protected.* No matter what name seems most life-giving to you—*soul, true self,* or *core beneath the core*—this part of me and you is real. It grows when it is noticed and when we practice habits that have evolved over millennia and that have served people facing the most terrifying ordeals. There is a reason great spiritual texts assure us we need not be afraid of those who can, as they say, "kill the body." There is a human core that cannot be touched by anyone except the soul that contains it. You can access this through practices as simple as sitting still and breathing quietly for a few minutes. All you need is a body and a place to sit. There are fathomless gifts and

---

* There are many beloved people who have taught this; among the best known are Viktor Frankl in *Man's Search for Meaning,* Maya Angelou in *I Know Why the Caged Bird Sings,* and Alice Walker in *The Color Purple.*

mysteries waiting for you to discover them. They constitute the real you, and they will grant you entrance to ever-deepening levels of authority over your own life. It's important to learn that the purpose of the core beneath the core is not to *separate* us from others but to properly *individuate each of us within an interdependent ecosystem* of people and other living beings. So discovering the core beneath the core can lead to the most profound communion with the other true selves you meet along the way. The best way I have found to describe this is that we find our place not as isolated selves but as welcome participants in the biggest story there is—the story of the evolution of love.

The impact you can have toward a better world is profoundly related to how much you fan the embers of this unimpactable part of yourself. It is possible, with grace and practice, for this *core beneath the core* to become indistinguishable from the self you present to the world.

I want to live unplagued by unnecessary fear, seeking wisdom and being tender toward myself and others. Even after the context that gave rise to our fear has faded away, fear may not respond to reason or changing circumstances alone. Fear is a spiritual condition, and it doesn't depend on external realities but on our perception of them. Plenty of people never experience real-world violence up close and personal but still live in fear. Plenty of us still think, *Surely I am going to be destroyed.*

But if we can change the burden of fear by reframing our perspective, the obvious starting point would be to ask ourselves one simple question: Why are we afraid in the first place?

An Invitation to Imagine a New Story

TAKE A FEW minutes to sit still and consider the following: The way you tell the story about your world will cocreate that world. This is true for the individual, everyday, and mundane details of your life as much as the cosmic, rare, and overwhelming scope of the universes we cannot see.

The story of violence bringing order out of chaos—which depends on fear and a lack of imagination—needs to be replaced. The personally diminishing story you tell about yourself, which is the only place your fear can exist, could likely use a comprehensive rewrite as well. Imagining a new story is a privilege. It is also our responsibility.

To take another step on the journey toward imagining a new story, consider three questions:

1. What resonates with you about the idea of imagining a new story?
2. What questions arise when you consider it?
3. What are some of the fears you're carrying?

chapter 3

a brief history
of fear

> What difference do it make if the
> thing you scared of is real or not?
>
> —Toni Morrison, *Song of Solomon*

THERE'S A SHORT and sweet story about where fear comes from and a longer and complicated one. The short and simple one has saber-toothed tigers in it, so let's start there.

Picture yourself in an era somewhere between the apes at the beginning of *2001: A Space Odyssey* and the Argonauts in Greek myth. You're wearing a rough cloth, grunting your answers, and driven by hunger and impulses to eat, sleep, procreate, and protect. You're living in a settlement of a couple dozen people, the original extended family. There is no king, no one's needs to serve but your own, and you share in community, though periodically you will probably participate in a raid on the settlement next door. Everything that matters takes place here.

There is also a saber-toothed tiger. Not a nice one. And when you're hunting monkeys or gathering leaves, you need to beware. While he does indeed burn bright, there is very little warning of his presence, and if you don't see him soon enough, you're toast (if you know what toast is). So when you sense the presence of this tiger, you run.

It's been a while now since we have had to contend with Shere Khan at our heels (and that *Jungle Book* tiger was as much a sly poetic manipulator as a pounce-and-tear-apart kind of beast). We have also begun to wean ourselves off the habit of seeing neighboring towns solely as a source of Others to kill or pillage.

Our brains, however, have inherited a legacy that owes more than a little to the presence of our saber-toothed friends. It's not just a memory; it's actually in our very bodies—most significantly, neuroscientists tell us, in the amygdalae, two groups of nuclei that look like almonds deep inside the intricate architecture of the brain. We're pretty sure that the amygdalae play a major role in triggering the fear response—the thudding heart, the tightness of the skin, the urge to run away or to lash out. We call this the fight-or-flight response, though this is not entirely accurate. In the third familiar option—freeze—fear is so overwhelming that it immobilizes us and we feel that we simply cannot move. At any rate, whether your amygdalae make you run away, fight back, or stand still, they evolved in response to the experience of danger.

In short, the reason you have two overly excitable almonds in your head is that thousands of years ago, Tony the Tiger confused your relatives with Frosted Flakes.

The tiger represents any number of dangers. Say humans had grown up in the west of Ireland; we might have evolved fear receptors from the experience of walking along the ridge of the Cliffs of Moher. This would have been reinforced by hearing stories of ancestors who fell to their deaths on the rocks below, either having not kept to the path or having been pushed off by ghosts. Regardless, whether we are afraid of cliff falls or tigers or something else, the point is the same: *fear is utterly natural.* The good news is that this means that human beings have developed a safety mechanism that is second to none. Better than any electronic early warning system, the amygdalae tell us when we need to protect ourselves and others. The bad news—or the challenge or the gift—is that the amygdalae can play a role in confusing us into thinking that *everything* is scary.

It's one thing to conceal yourself or flee when you *know* that a predator or potential cliff fall is nearby. That's when fear looks a lot like wisdom. It's comforting to know that there's something embedded in our bodies that causes the heightened sense of awareness that can prevent us from coming to harm in such settings.

The problem is that the amygdalae do not accurately discern the *nature* or *scale* of the danger. Only stories do that. We may see a flash of orange-and-black fur behind some trees, a shine of teeth, or even hear a tropical growl. But unless we adjust our eyes and discern a narrative, we won't know if the tiger is Shere Khan or Tony or Tigger or Hobbes. Human beings predict the probability of something happening based on how easily we can remember similar things, and many of us live in a culture addicted to telling stories of terrible things as if they are the *only* things. So we're liable to inflate the implications of what's lurking in the bushes.

I don't know about you, but Tigger and Hobbes don't scare me. In fact, I'm sure I'd enjoy spending time with them. Hobbes is wise and funny, and Tiggers are, of course, wonderful things. If I let my amygdalae do all the talking, though, I might be mounting their heads as trophies on the wall instead of spending the afternoon bouncing around with them.

An amygdala is an unreliable narrator. Look no further than those tragic incidents of parents shooting a presumed burglar in the dark before making the awful discovery that it was one of their own children frightened by the storm outside. There is a difference between the impulse triggered by the amygdalae and the story we must learn: that *most* of our fears are not true at all and that *all* of them depend on a story we tell ourselves. We might estimate that, say, 10 percent of our fears are somehow rooted in reality—tigers and cliffs and the potential damage done by having 120 horsepower under the control of your right foot. Fear is therefore a gift of nature. It has already saved your life more times than you can count.

But fear cannot control itself. We often either exaggerate the unrealistic threats or seem unable to hold the story that while realistic ones may hurt, they cannot annihilate our truest selves. Every mind needs to be trained to tell the difference between the wisdom of avoiding tigers and the waste of fearing things that are not there. If we don't learn how to transform it, fear will control us. If we become preoccupied or even obsessed with fearing things that either aren't real or are much smaller than fear tells us, we will fall into a dangerous trap. A life wasted on protecting ourselves from things that can't harm the soul is a misdirected life, perhaps even a squandered one. A life wasted on protecting *parts* of us that don't matter from things that aren't real is an unlived life.

Without the spiritual discipline of healthy storytelling, fear can be like mercury set free to colonize every cranny of a plastic maze. How we remember things, where we perceive ourselves to be today, and the vantage point from which we view the future will determine whether fear controls us. It doesn't have to.

We each have our personal triggers: words and events that remind us of pain or fear and cause us to wince or worse. But to be triggered means that we have heart enough to care about our pain—that we are not dead inside. It is possible to transform our triggers into reminders that we are not, after all, trapped in an overwhelming past or imagined future. With healing attention, we can—and this is one of the most astonishing things— develop the superpower of letting our triggers catapult us *into the present.* We can learn to distinguish the wisdom that protects and energizes from the fictions that do nothing but confuse and frighten. More than that, we can even learn to transform fear into a reminder of how to find our proper place among the miracles that surround us all the time.

TIGERS IN THE wild represent at least two miraculous unveilings about the nature of the world and about what it is to be human. Human-eating predators, the poetic naturalist David Quammen tells us, are a gift to the circle of life. In their natural habitat, they do what must be done. When interfered with, they don't discern that the interruption has come from human beings with souls and families, so hunters of rare game shouldn't take it personally if Tony bites back. It seems likely that the great white shark would never come so close to shore as to eat humans if we hadn't stripped his deep-sea fish stocks of food through misguided notions of industrial growth at all costs. Though such natural predators may induce fear, they offer us the gift of humility. There are creatures that might eat us, but if we would leave them alone, they would ignore us. The glory of nature is partly that when we work *with* the ecosystem, it works with us. We are foolish to think we can dominate the earth or that we ever needed to in the first place.

There is another beautiful gift to be had in recognizing our interdependence with others in the ecosystem. Human beings have the responsibility of stewardship when it comes to the natural world, but that doesn't mean we own it. For one thing, we are not separate from but *part* of the ecosystem. This fact should be obvious but is usually not acknowledged. Some see such humility as a threat or an insult. Yet the gift of our place in the food chain is the gift of exchanging conquest for stewardship. People who exploit the ecosystem for profit might consider how much more enjoyable their lives would be if they didn't believe that everything else depended on them. Indeed, knowing that there really *are* things that are worth being afraid of—or things that should at least inspire the wisdom of discernment—is a gift. Reflecting on how nature (or perhaps the sacred) has figured out that we need a little help, a little guidance on the tricky path of being alive, is the deepest comfort.

The responsibility of our place in the food chain is to recognize, as Quammen says, that when tigers are "lost from the wild, they're lost in the deepest sense." Some fear is healthy because it helps us make wise choices, protect ourselves and others, and become good stewards of the earth and its resources. This is freedom: to discern possibility and danger and decide what to do with them. Without this freedom, we would be little more than robots.

The human being is an ecosystem too, and there is a miraculous interdependence within the structure of our bodies, minds, and true selves. A little fear can actually help grant us the most human quality of all: the ability to choose. This may be why one of our most archetypal fears is the fear of authorities, who sometimes claim that they can take our choices away.

I HAVE NEVER liked the idea of "authorities." Where I come from, so many of our rules emerged to keep our society stuck in "us" and "them" silos that I suppose I had reason to be wary of those who think they know how to run things. We knew not to go to certain places lest we get caught up in violence or a bomb scare, public authority was contested, and the ambiguous status of the state we were in made the powers that be seem even more unreachable. The fear of power being exercised without compassion or force being imposed without accountability was palpable.

Most of us know what it's like to tense up after seeing a police car concealed on an interstate median while driving faster than the sign says we should. Some of us experience far more serious disadvantages than mere internal anxiety arising from the systemic disregard or even active disdain for our race, gender, sexual orientation, citizenship status, bodily condition, education, or age, often manifesting in the form of genuine lack. Many of us have experienced the fear that we might be accused of something we did not do and not be able to defend ourselves, and of course the structural realities behind that fear are more dangerous for some of us than others.

To take a mundane example, otherwise emotionally mature and confident individuals have been known to worry when the mail arrives, in case a letter from the tax authorities or a past-due bill is among the letters. A wise archbishop once said that if approached by a stranger on the street who whispers, "They know. Run!" most of us would indeed flee. We give so much power to the invisible authorities that they have some hold over every one of us—which returns us to how the isolating strategy of fear is self-defeating. If *all* of us are afraid of something, then maybe there are reasons to believe the lonely part of the fear just a little bit less.

There is an invisible system of authority in the world. An ancient Middle Eastern text calls it "principalities and powers"; sociologists call it the "social structure"; others just call it "the way things are." In *The Grapes of Wrath*, John Steinbeck wrote a perfect metaphor for the shadow side of power when one of his characters considers how a bank may be "made of men" but that still "men can't control it." The men from the bank come to tell the men on the farm that they have no jobs anymore because the bank has decided it's not profitable. The men have sweated and died working the land; the bank has never even seen the land.

We've all observed what theologian and biblical scholar Walter Wink calls the "domination system" at work—in war, in retribution, in discrimination and other injustices, or in any situation where personal, humane interaction is short-circuited by bureaucracy. This cannot be denied: the world is burdened by the often stumbling, sometimes cruel behavior of human beings. And whether on the floor of the United Nations General

Assembly, where nationalistic self-interest can blind decent people to the common good, or in a restaurant, where a server must fend off the insults of customers dissatisfied with something over which the server has no control, shadow power operates when we choose the inauthenticity of isolation over the integrity of love.

At the same time, humans predict the probability of bad events occurring based on how easily we can remember stories of similar things. In other words, the more we think about something, the more likely we predict it will happen again. This means that it's no surprise when people living in an information culture addicted to bad news predict that the letter from the government will be a traffic fine and not a tax rebate. More seriously, the imposition of authority without consent heightens legitimate fears among people with less access to the center of institutional power.

It is a broken world, but on the path to repair, we see so many examples of how power can be used with love. Mercy can be shown, gentle warnings can be given, curiosity and education can replace judgment and scorn. Power—from how we run cities and public safety services to how entire nations relate to each other and how human beings relate to the entire planet—can be shared interdependently and exercised with mutual respect for the thriving of all life. But other people's choices won't matter as much if you nurture the supreme authority within because the only yes that can really mean yes (or no that can mean no, or maybe that can mean maybe) is that which proceeds from your true self. This part of you is likely somewhat buried, because our culture doesn't typically do a good job of introducing the ego to the true self. You've likely had decades of building a persona based on what other people told you, from parents to friends to teachers to politics to religion to all kinds of cultural systems. There were probably elements of the story that were kind, connecting, creative, and courageous, but when the heart of the story was selfishness, scapegoating, and separation, there was probably part of you that resisted it. If you encountered wise mentors among the storytellers in your life, you may well have been initiated into the discovery of the true self.

But if you're like most of us, your true self has been a quiet voice inside, the one that pushes back against what's so obviously wrong in the world, pursues the path of wholeness even when it's unpopular, secretly weeps when you see a rainbow, is willing to die but not kill, knows that there is something real beyond what we have been trained to see with our eyes, something indescribably good. That part may be buried, but it's real.

The reason that it's hard to find can be partly explained by the longer and more complicated story about where fear comes from. There are no tigers in it. There don't need to be any tigers—because in this story, we learn the lie that the monster is us.

ONE OF THE most provocative theories about the inner life— and the longer and more complicated story of fear's origins— comes from the French philosopher Michel Foucault's writings on the development of the self. Foucault explains how fear-inducing authorities taught us how to understand ourselves through a fascinating observation: that, at least in cultures dominated by Christendom, humans took a leap forward in defining ourselves through the repetition of confessing our sins to a priest, to whom we ascribed the very power of God. Thus we reinforced the notions that what is most important about ourselves is a bunch of things we are ashamed of (or that we have been told we *should* be ashamed of). This story taught us that to feel ashamed is a "sacrament" and therefore good for us and that there is a higher power who is more interested in punishing our mistakes than in affirming our beauty.

Keeping guilt and fear bottled up inside is no good for any of us. As Leonard Cohen says, the crack is where the light gets in, so it's worth noting that healthy confession—in conversation with an emotionally mature, nonshaming confessor—is indeed good for the soul. There is healing in facing our inner darkness and making amends. Healthy confession includes the liberation of knowing you're not alone, the opportunity to learn from your mistakes, and the forging of new agreements so you can walk a little taller next time.

But unhealthy models of confession, Foucault contends, have created the self as a little shame receptacle, unable to take responsibility for its actions and needing a magician in the sky to pronounce it clean. Many people experience confession merely as a mental checklist or a superficial game, a kind of spiritual tallying we employ to feel better about ourselves or because it fits the norms of the community we're desperately hoping will accept us. The lenses through which we identify "sin" or "darkness" derive from the whims of the authorities. This means giving away what Simone Weil called our greatest power: the power to say "I."

Given the power we cede to religious and other authorities as our surrogate decision-makers, many of us have inherited shame-filled notions about ourselves, and we have a lot of unlearning to do about when to surrender power and when to take it. Confession, for me, was first equated with naming my darkness rather than my light, my shadow rather than my gold. As a result, I am prone to overread the darkness and curse it rather than noticing the million candles already lit. Some say we become what we pay attention to. It's no wonder, then, that when my vision was restricted by the culture of confessing only the shadow, darkness was all I could see. It's no wonder that I thought I was ugly and greeted the concept of innocence as a sign of weakness rather than understanding innocence as a sign of the true immensity of what it is to be human. As both beginning *and* destiny.

WE ALL HAVE the experience of an authority figure or institution of whom we've been afraid. For some of us, it's a parent, whose love became confused and twisted in harsh discipline or whose own brokenness had not been tended and who acted out their shadow on us. For some it is a religious culture that bound us up in ropes, tightly knotted at one end but with enough freedom of movement that we could flagellate ourselves with the other—a culture in which well-meaning people were still transmitting the dehumanizing and broken ideas about original sin and the depravity of children. For some it is the fear that the authorities will break their promises or of systems that enforce the heresy that some lives are worth more than others. Some recoil from the very image or idea of God. And that's OK—knowing these things allows you to begin to be gentle with yourself.

So let me say something more about God—or, if I'm to be accurate, *God*. The word cannot contain what it seeks to convey. No word can, but let's face it, *God* is one of the biggest—so big that its very gravity is easily disregarded. It's too hot to handle. We do so much *talking* about *God* without ever touching the wisdom of the concept, never mind experiencing it. So let's try this: I don't think God is a cuddly bloke with a nice beard, sitting in the clouds. But I do think that if you find that image life-giving, you are welcome to it, and may it bring you joy. When I use the word *God*, I mean something like what is conveyed by the phrase "Reality with a capital *R* and more."

Let's imagine that God is Reality and that Reality is bigger than the universes, known and unknown; it is the Ground of Being, which itself initiates the very possibility that we could imagine anything at all. God induces the rules of logic and reason, is the explanation of everything, permeates every molecule, and is almost completely revealed in every human face. Pure Love.

You have been born into a world full of people trying to get it right but whose imperfect conclusions gave you a gift: the need to figure things out for yourself. So you get the chance to consciously choose how you will participate in the next stage of human evolution rather than parroting the mistakes of the past. (Apologies to any parrots who may be reading. I'm sure you have something original to say too.)

What that conscious choosing looks like, of course, is up to you. It can be no other way. Fear of external authorities can only be transcended by the human being taking authority for herself. Imagination, in the end, may be the only thing that cannot be held prisoner except with the prisoner's consent. The bittersweet opportunity for you, for me, for everyone we know is to realize we are our own jailers. And from your jail, where you shackle yourself to a vision of the world that ascribes power to invisible spiritual forces that can create wars, poverty, political oppression, and the DMV, the amazing gift is that no one holds the key to your prison but you. You can take steps to free yourself by nurturing the authoritative voice within. In fact, nurturing authority within is the first step toward overcoming fear.

Consider this: If you lack mercy for yourself, imagine becoming more merciful to others. Do it for long enough, and you will start to forgive yourself.

If you are a harsh critic, offer yourself feedback by first identifying what you did well and then identifying one suggestion for a better way to do it next time—without dwelling on what you think you did badly.

If your community tends to curse the darkness before lighting candles, consider buying some candles.

If you have given power over your own life to external authorities, try to retrace the journey that led you there and take back one piece of power at a time.

If you need help, learn how—and from whom—to ask for it.

IT'S A PARADOX that the path to overcoming fear depends on discovering the true self because that requires walking through the very vulnerability that may have us afraid in the first place. We may be afraid to face our true selves. The good news is that it doesn't have to happen all at once; in fact, it's a lifetime path. But if we pay attention to the wisdom found in stories about this path, we can choose moments, sometimes every day, that can dissolve the force field so many of us find between us and who we really are. Here are a couple of stories that might help.

When I was not long out of college, I needed to borrow money from my dad. I borrowed £1,000—about $1,600 at the time—and made an agreement that I would pay it back on a certain date.

But I couldn't pay it back, and as the day approached, I was weighed down by the fear of telling Dad as well as the pressure of the story I was telling myself about my financial circumstances. I did not try to do anything about my situation, which is a typical response to the fear trigger: the tiger is coming at us, so we freeze and squeeze our eyes tight. It's that adorably futile hope that not being able to see will somehow make us invisible.

I went over to see Dad on a Saturday morning. He was expecting a repayment. I was expecting D-Day. We sat at opposite ends of the kitchen table as I told him the truth: not only could I not pay him back that day, but I needed to borrow more money.

Two remarkable things ensued. The first was that as my dad told me, tears welling, that he did not have any more money in the bank to lend, I took another step toward adulthood. Toward taking authority for myself. He was no longer the invincible god upon whom I relied—and who I blamed—for everything, but a man, beautiful and vulnerable, just like me.

The second was that in the very same moment, he embodied the kind of grace, generosity, and tenderness that only authentic authority figures can. After leaving the room for a few minutes to think about what should be done—while I stewed in anxiety in the kitchen—he returned with a smile. A few months prior, I had loaned him my bicycle, which I did not like or use and which he himself had given me in the first place. It was worth about £80. My dad said he really didn't have any more money he could loan at the time, but he really liked my bike, and if it would be OK with me, he wanted to purchase it from me. He said he thought it was worth about £1,000, and if that price were acceptable to me, we could just call it even. So we did. It was an enormous gift, a healing moment, which not only took away my anxiety but saved us both from shame.

We live in a powerful moment of possibility. Vulnerability is gradually becoming more valued as a way of being, even in public life. This is a tender plant needing nurture, and given that shaming, not mercy, has been a go-to mode for so long, I think we should declare help-askers the heroes of our time. The very request for help should be an occasion for rejoicing, for another human being is setting themselves free from the death-dealing oppression that says we are alone and must fend for ourselves. So much violence proceeds from someone needing help but feeling unable to ask for it. Three of the largest genocides of the twentieth century proceeded from the unresolved brokenness of just three individuals: Adolf Hitler, Joseph Stalin, and Pol Pot. Can you imagine a world in which any of them had been initiated into asking for help to discern what he really needed?

Think about the times that you have experienced debilitating fear. I'm willing to bet that the thing that you thought was going to happen probably didn't. Or if it did, it wasn't nearly as bad as you expected. Or if it was, you can at least claim today you are a survivor. The most likely truth is that you were not afraid primarily of the thing itself but of your ability to cope with the thing if it happened.

Another way of putting this would be to say that you were afraid not so much of the threat but of yourself. The gift of fearing the authorities is the opportunity to deepen your authority within yourself. And there's a special bonus prize: sometimes the authorities end up healed too.

A FRIEND OF mine often told a story about a man condemned to spend a night in a dark cell with a poisonous snake. All night he cowered in the corner, trying not to breathe for fear that he would rouse his slinky executioner. The terror was such that he thought the fear itself might kill him; there'd be no need for the serpent to bite.

When dawn began to break through the cell window, he did not allow himself to hope that he would soon be released and free from danger in case he let out a sound that would seal his fate at the last minute. Perhaps his moment of greatest fear was when he heard the guard's footsteps in the corridor on his way to open the door and let him go. Silently praying that the jangle of the guard's keys would not waken the snake, he observed sunlight creeping across the floor, redoubling his fear. Wouldn't the snake be woken by the brightness? But the light had a different effect, for just as the guard unlocked the door, the condemned man saw that the monstrous snake in the cell was not, in fact, a snake at all. It was a piece of old rope coiled in the corner. An object for the purpose of teaching spiritual growth to people in his town.

Sure, it's comforting to know that the thing that terrifies us is usually just a piece of old rope in the corner. But the important thing about this story is that the condemned man just accepted his fate. He could have asked questions of the authorities who put him in the cell; he could have researched snakes; he could have asked for help; he could even have talked to the snake. He didn't do this because he was afraid—not of the snake or of the authorities but of himself, because he had handed over his own will to someone else. He had surrendered his will to false authorities because he had not learned to have authority over himself.

As I've mentioned, we are justified in our fears to a much lower level than what we imagine; much of the time our fears may be entirely without foundation. And even for those fears that are based in reality, most human experience teaches us that going through something we were terrified of is often less terrible than the fear itself. The experience of fear can be so debilitating that we actually end up *forgetting* what it is we are afraid of. The way fear seizes our minds and bodies is sometimes so powerful, it may seem as if there is no filter between our fear and our very *selves*.

One of my friends would nurture the gift of quieting his soul enough to ask himself, "What is it *exactly* that I'm afraid of?" Sometimes he would do this over and over again until he got to the root of his fear. It was always something smaller than his emotions were telling him. He realized that his fears could not be bigger than him. If he was experiencing them, then they existed *inside* him, which meant *he* was bigger than his fear. And asking, with surgical precision, the exact nature of his fears allowed for the possibility of taking some control over the circumstances that gave rise to them.

There are probably bits of old rope in each of our lives that we confuse with poisonous snakes. We imagine the snake in the corner, and we fight with both the snake and the fears of what it might do to us. We put ourselves into a perpetual struggle with an imaginary snake. There's a Hopi invocation that, among other things, asks us to "banish the word 'struggle' from [our] attitude and [our] vocabulary." That's a variation on what I want to do with fear: not to eradicate it but to allow it to find its proper balance. This means not only reducing its power by paring away its unnecessary excess but asking just what lesson the old rope in the corner wants to teach me.

An Invitation to Consider What Gives You Life

THE WAY WE wake up in the morning, how we prepare and eat meals, the way we go to work, how we wash the dishes (or let them pile up), how we park the car or go to the movies, what we wear to weddings or on holiday or at home: we all engage in rituals, whether we call them *rituals* or not. Brian McLaren defines *ritual* as "an act that employs the body to bond to a meaning." Rituals include our patterns of relating to others: loved ones, friends, colleagues, strangers, people we don't like, people we fear. Just how much and in what ways we interact with (or are controlled by) technology—email, social media, the "news"—may be the most surprising facts of our ritual lives. What are your rituals?

There is an old spiritual practice that people have found helpful in transforming their rituals from those that keep us spiritually asleep into ones that animate our lives as extraordinary journeys. Consider a typical day or even a week in your life and note the repeated patterns. Then ask yourself two questions:

1. Which of these ritual practices are life-giving?
2. Which of these ritual practices bring less life—or worse, even bring a kind of death?

Make two lists, one for each type: life-giving rituals and death-dealing rituals. Then do fewer of the death-dealing rituals and more of the life-giving ones. This practice will help you discover your truer self.

chapter 4

you don't know the end of the story

> There is no real ending. It's just
> the place where you stop the story.
>
> —Frank Herbert

I REMEMBER STANDING on a platform giving a talk to five hundred Serious Religious People about sectarianism in Ireland. I was privileged to be there and couldn't quite believe that I had been invited. As I championed amends for ancient enmities and, with a bit of mischief, summoned the gall to confront the empire, the crowd clapped and laughed in the right places. They lined up afterward to tell me how good it had been, and someone even referred to it as a "historic moment" in the life of that already very historic institution.

Yet while I was on the stage riffing on my prepared text, showing slides, and politely sipping my glass of water, the voice in my head was not proud or quietly confident. It was terrified. It was buzzing, *You're not good enough. And everybody knows it. You're going to be destroyed.*

Buzzing is apt because these thoughts are like bees: they encircle my mind, and every now and then, they sting. It starts in my chest with a tightening. My legs feel unstable. My temples ache. I get the not-nice kind of goose bumps. My head tries to turn away, repelled by what it thinks it can see. I spiral downward into the fear that nothing I can do will atone for the mistakes of the past and forward into the melancholic fog that threatens that I'll keep repeating the same mistakes forever or that terrible things will happen to me.

This foreboding stabs me in the sternum, a dart. Though I attempt self-psychotherapy, my body and mind are seized by terror, luxuriating in distractions and plummeting into darkness. *I left the gas stove lit or the door unlocked* quickly becomes *I'm going to go bankrupt*. Then it's only a skip and a jump to *I'll never be happy, I'll never be at home,* or *I'm going to be the victim of violence*. And then, before long, it comes to *I'm going to be destroyed—along with the rest of the world*.

Over time, these notions have become intimate with my inner landscape. I've rehearsed them even as the person visible to the outside world has seemed gentle, funny, and happy. I can play the game with the crowd to impress them or just to keep myself afloat. I have learned ways of accepting these little voices. I have visited with them so often that their torments are second nature.

There are good reasons that my psyche latched onto the idea that something awful was going to happen to me. As I said earlier, I was formed in a place where awful things always seemed to be happening, so much so that the story of our place seemed to be that awful things were the *only* things happening—or at least the most likely. The violent civil conflict in northern Ireland was presented as *the story* of our lives. In some senses, we *inhabited* violence because our very identities were explained to us in oppositional—or at least defensive—terms. Many of us believed, or acted like we believed, that triumphal denunciation or physical humiliation of the other would keep us strong. We embodied the myth of redemptive violence, acting as if denying the needs of people who were different would both erase them *and* (re)establish our nation. Even in the parts of this story that were grounded in ideas about safety or health or pride, in the end, we were also feeding the beast that wanted to devour us.

We were victims of what social scientists call the *availability bias*: the way human beings predict the probability of something happening based on how easily we recall similar things. We were surrounded by violence, or at least that's what our culture told us. We were also surrounded by hospitality and green fields and laughter and kindness, but those stories don't usually make the news, so we believed that violence was our way of life. The availability bias worked on us, limiting our sense of possibility to a gruesome hall of mirrors. And we bought it—partly because we didn't understand it and partly because it is a natural response to genuine trauma to want to hide in a corner. There was pressure to live as if everything was going to hell, that we were basically the last people on a life raft trying to make sure that no one else weighed it down, that no one could be trusted, and that we were always right.

This kind of thinking is very costly. Seamus Heaney evoked the feeling of presumptive mistrust that northern Irish people lived with in his phrase "whatever you say, say nothing." Not being able to talk honestly with others makes it easy to develop an overactive voice in your own head. Of course, that voice doesn't emerge only in people who grew up surrounded by political tension and shadows. Among other journeys, it also comes to those who have to navigate the discovery of not being "straight" in a culture of anti-LGBTQ prejudice.

So I spent my childhood talking to myself. Talking myself into believing that I was in danger all the time and that because I was different, there was something wrong with me. You can, of course, *choose* to visit your little torturers and thereby maintain some facsimile of control. But unless you're doing it as part of something therapeutic like intentional shadow work, properly facilitated, this is only as wise as the alcoholic who tells himself that he can have *just one drink* and it'll be fine.

For some reason, I have never found it easy to keep things bottled up inside, and at any rate, my fear was so painful that I couldn't ignore it. I have always been a talker, so I also talked to anyone who would listen, inking my anxiety onto the blotting paper I perceived my fellow human beings to be. Perception turned out to be important because it was not ultimately the wound or the traumatic effects of the wound that were the problem. It was how I thought about them.

I know this because a Swiss Armed Forces veteran once asked me to share a cigarillo with him under the Eiffel Tower. I have told this story countless times because I need to remember its gift. Although I first received it over two decades ago, the gift still evolves today.

IN THE SUMMER of 1997, I found myself in Paris for one night only. It was the end of a month's travels around the continent by train: eating Nepalese food in Amsterdam and baguettes and cheese in Geneva, seeing New York films in Prague, climbing up the tower with the angel statue in Berlin, taking Lutheran Eucharist on the streets of Oslo, dancing in Barcelona, standing still in Auschwitz. I had a day free before my flight home, so I did what all right-thinking aspirational hipster Euro-railers would do. I took a train to the most romantic city in the world and went down to its most recognizable tourist trap: the Eiffel Tower, so familiar from a dozen disaster movie clips wherein the tower's collapse or explosion or flooding or vaporization serves as a proxy for the imminent colonization of Europe by aliens, meteorites, or Godzillas. It was, of course, also the emblem of Ilsa and Rick's love in *Casablanca*; they would "always have Paris," and this same thought would eventually guide me to a place of perpetual comfort.

For the story played by Ingrid Bergman and Humphrey Bogart in the 1942 film turns out to be as transcendent a parable as many in the more conventional sacred texts. At the climax of *Casablanca*, by choosing the path where each can be of most service to the common good, Ilsa and Rick give up the hope of a life physically present together. But their love will always sustain itself, even across time and distance. That's what "We'll always have Paris" means. That at the end of the day, because nothing real is ever lost, we don't have to choose between remaining grounded in our truest self or stepping into transformation. If love is the energy that animates us, we can stay exactly who we always were (in all the ways that matter most) and still change (evolving toward a deeper experience of those very same things). But I didn't know that yet. I was just visiting the Eiffel Tower with a pack of Cohiba cigarillos in my pocket, which at that point in my twenty-two-year-old life was probably the most expensive single-item purchase I had yet made. It was a ten-pack of the small cigars, made in Cuba, and which I smoked with the kind of effort a novice like me had to exert in order to make something look effortless. By the time I got to Paris, there were five cigarillos left in the pack.

The admission fee to the tower was beyond my remaining coins I had after a month of budget travel, so I lay on my back underneath it, gazing up at the gorgeous, oversized Meccano from within, imagining myself as if I had just been born and was looking back at where I came from. I was about to be born again.

I wandered down to one of the bridges near the tower, the Pont de l'Alma, and sat by the Seine. I lit up cigarillo number six and smoked it like the insecure northern Irish recovering evangelical that I was: scared of everything, including myself, and trying to hide it. A man approached carrying the unmistakable aroma of someone who hasn't been able to wash in awhile. He asked if he could have a cigarillo, and I obliged. I knew enough French for us to be able to carry one side of a little conversation, so we talked awhile.

His name was Jean-Marc, and he had come to Paris from Switzerland five months earlier, after spending time in the army. He had fallen on hard times, and now he was living outside. "Paris only cares about tourists," he told me. "She doesn't care about her own people." He cried a little when he said this. He avoided my eyes while talking, looking toward the river.

Time did what time does, and soon enough, it was time for me to take the last metro home. So I asked him if I could give him some money, but he declined. Then I asked if there was anything else I could give him, gritting my teeth and quietly hoping that he would not request the remaining three cigarillos. Mid-grit, another thought came to me: *Give to those who ask of you.* It was someone else's thought, of course, but one of the gifts of the evangelicalism from which I was recovering was that such good teachings were never far from my mind, even if they were not uniformly practiced. Jean-Marc did indeed want the cigarillos, and I gave them with a secret grimace. He reached into his backpack and took out a set of electric hair clippers that he told me he had found on the street. He handed them to me as a trade. He grabbed my shoulders and embraced me, kissing me on the cheeks the way French people do.

And then he pulled my face close to his and kissed me full on the lips, lingering. I tasted his beer and his stubble, and I saw his eyes up close as he held my face in his hands. Moving back a couple of inches, he said, "Je n'ai pas le SIDA. Je vous fais plaisir?" Only today do I notice that after telling me that he did not have AIDS, he used the formal form of "you" in offering to have sex with me for money. I can still see his dark and lovely eyes and hear his earlier tears, the sniffle after telling me how his adopted city did not care about him.

We awkwardly found a way out of that conversation. I took the metro back to the flat where I was staying that night—and I told the story of Jean-Marc for years to come.

Initially I told it as an illustration of how religious folks often hold our beliefs as if they were a kind of "truth missile," approaching people we consider to be Other as if *they* are the targets. As if only *we* have something to give *them*, as if *they* have nothing to give *us* except their acquiescence. For years I told the story of meeting Jean-Marc as a provocation to people like me to stop acting as if everyone else is merely a receptacle for our spiritual "wisdom," as if Jean-Marc were just a plaything for my ego. If we approach people as unwitting potential sectarian recruits, it should be no surprise that sometimes they react as if we're carrying out an economic transaction. When you build relationships on othering, you learn more about math than love.

Telling the story that way carried me through lots of seminars, conferences, and one-to-one conversations about peacemaking and othering, not to mention providing an indulgence for my ego. You can only tell a story in which you are the hero for so long before you discover either that you aren't one or that some act of actual heroism will eventually be required of you. One of the strangest gifts of life is that stories we tell about ourselves can sometimes contain the seeds of exactly what we need in the future, even if we don't understand them the first time around.

It took fourteen years for my day of the most gentle reckoning.

When the Cohibas found me again, I was giving my little talk in a church in North Carolina, relying on the story of Jean-Marc and the cigarillos in Paris to illustrate my point about religion and identity and transactional relating when the pastor stood up and exited the room. Knocked off my game, I struggled to bring the talk in for a soft landing. The pastor was gone only a few minutes, and I was relieved on his return to see that he was beaming. He held a wooden box. He took the stage, thanked me, handed me the box, and said, "I think these are yours."

His friend had been in Cuba the previous week and returned with a gift, in a lovely wooden box, of three Cohiba cigars. They had been traveling for almost a decade and a half, across an ocean, generously expanding to Churchillian proportions, to find me in a church in a part of the country I was adopting, just so that I could be hit by this lightning: I am living a story-in-progress.

We're *all* living a story-in-progress.

Our identities are formed and re-formed through the way we construct and revise the story: the version we tell ourselves, the version we tell others, the version we fear is true, and the version we hope for. The way we receive and hold on to our memories is the foundation of the story. By paying some attention and doing some work to reframe our memories, we can alter that foundation, remaking it for our own healing.

The first way I framed the story of Paris and Jean-Marc and Cohiba cigarillos, it ended in the summer of 1997. But fourteen years later, the same cigarillos—both in brand and in number—and I arrived in the same place at the same time, and the story was forever changed. It's still a story in which I learned that othering people makes for transactional relationships rather than those founded on love.

But that's not the heart of the story. The heart of the story is a point about stories themselves. And the point is this: *you never know when a story is over, especially if you're in it.*

TWO YEARS AFTER the cigars caught up with me, a friend suggested that I was *still* missing the point. In listening to him, I saw that the story had come to mean something so profound that if it were not true, I would consider it bad writing. My friend told me that, yes, it's good to try to wean ourselves off the patronizing and sectarian thinking that leads us to treat people as Other; it's good to move beyond transaction and into relationship. Sure, it's great that we can reinterpret those stories, especially given that our identities are shaped by the stories we're telling. Especially because we can never know when a story is over. Especially if we're in it. It is indeed a seed of the healing of the human race—not to mention the planet—to learn that we suffer when we believe our thoughts are carved into rock—or are even the rock itself. Yet none of our thoughts are immutable, and all of our stories can be told anew, every single day, meeting our pain with curiosity, sometimes transforming our suffering into wonder.

Yes, these are brilliant lessons, and how lovely it is that I have a little story to tell that is two parts fun, one part pathos, and illustrates these liberative notions. But still, my friend said, you're missing the point. "Sixteen years ago, something happened to you that everyone wants to have happen to them," he said. "It's the archetype of romance. It's something people fantasize about but never believe they could actually have. And you not only got to have it, but for sixteen years, you haven't even noticed."

I still didn't, so I asked him, "What is this thing I've been missing?"

"It's simple," he said. "You were kissed by a beautiful stranger under the Eiffel Tower."

I'VE THOUGHT ABOUT Jean-Marc many times in the more than twenty years since we met. I don't, of course, know where he is, how he is, or even if he is still alive. I am grateful for what he helped me learn. After telling and retelling the story of our meeting on a balmy Parisian night, I have found at least three things to be true:

You never know when a story is over, especially if you're in it.
You never really know what the story is about, even if you're the protagonist.
And you might not know the point of a story, even if you're the one telling it.

If you're living through difficult times, it may be of some comfort to you to remember previous difficult times in which your perception of an ending from which you could not recover turned out to be mistaken. An apparent dead end concealed a doorway. And if you can't be certain of the point of a story even if you're the one telling it, you have endless possibilities to reframe your own life and liberate yourself from old paradigms of fear by imagining a different way of understanding and telling your own story.

There's always more going on than we know—and if you're in despair for the failure of your attempts at "fixing" your fear, consider this: it's not true to say that we have tried everything and none of it works, for none of us could possibly know what everything is. Accepting the fact of not knowing is one way to help ease our fear. So in the effort of expanding your own possibilities, don't just play around with the *ending* of your story; try experimenting with the *cast*. Are you really at the center of all the stories of fear you tell yourself? Are you the hero—or the victim—of every story you're telling? Really? That response may seem natural and utterly obvious, but I'm not so certain anymore. I'll tell you this for sure: I'm not the protagonist of Jean-Marc's story.

When the Italian mystic St. Francis kissed a man suffering from leprosy instead of rejecting him, an entire branch of Christian theology and practice was advanced. Francis became the icon for people seeking to serve among the most marginalized people, and this is, of course, a wonderful thing. All respect to Brother Francis.

But we never hear what happened to the guy with leprosy he kissed. He is just left by the side of the road, a launching point for revelation in the life of Francis and a sermon illustration that has lasted almost a millennium. But as my husband, Brian, says, "What's in it for the leper?"

What, indeed? It's a beautiful troubling of the waters to consider that in this story, I may actually be the leper rather than St. Francis. Or I may be St. Francis, but with a serious ego problem. In any case, I may not be the protagonist at all.

This has tremendous implications for how we experience fear. If we never know when a story is over, especially when we're in it, we can't assert that our fears will hold the final card. There is always room for a surprise.

It's a good idea to hold our stories of fear loosely. Shake them out from time to time, like sand-permeated beach towels. Turn them upside down, look at them from a different angle. Even if the stories we're telling are true and helpful, they can always use a tune-up. On the other hand, if they're less true or less helpful, they might benefit from a complete overhaul.

So let's not assume we know what even our most cherished stories mean. The truth is, we *never* know what other people really thought or think of us, the true impact of our actions or inactions, what's around the next corner, if we have fifty years or ten minutes left to live. Letting ourselves rest in not knowing is a tremendous relief from an exhausting and futile attempt at ruling the world.

If I am not the protagonist, my ego no longer has to hold the burden of being at the center of the story. But who or what is? And if there is indeed a better story with a better center, how can I find it?

An Invitation to Name Your Stories

WE CAN'T CHANGE our stories if we don't know what they are. Shaping the story we're telling about our lives is one of the most important things we'll ever do, but we usually do it unconsciously. We so often take the "facts" for granted and don't question the context or imagine alternatives. If your story is killing you, poisoning others, holding you hostage to someone else's dreams or nightmares, or merely holding you *back* from living your truest self, consider an intervention.

You might try sitting still for ten minutes and begin to explore the elements of the story you tell yourself—some of the following questions might help:

What is the story you tell yourself about who you are, what matters about your life, what was done to you, or what you did in return? About your hopes, dreams, wounds, complaints? Write down or sketch the responses that emerge.

What stories have you been told about your name? About your family? About your nation? About who the "good guys" and the "bad guys" are? About what you should hope for in life?

Question those stories, one plot point at a time. Is it true? Is it helpful? Is there a truer or more helpful version of this story?

If you could change the story you tell about yourself—past, present, and future—and still tell the truth, who might you become?

chapter 5

your story can be a shelter

There is something in every one of you that waits and listens for the sound of the genuine in yourself. It is the only *true* guide you will ever have. And if you cannot hear it, you will all of your life spend your days on the ends of strings that somebody else pulls.

—Howard Thurman

I ONCE JOINED forty people walking up a west of Ireland mountain under torrential rain. When we reached the top, all forty squeezed into a stone shelter, and as we rested there, I told a story. Before we arrived at the shelter, we were tired and wet and cold and annoyed, perhaps even fearful that we would ever get where we were supposed to be going. Looking back, however, I see that the shelter not only removed us from the hardship of the rain; it changed the way we thought about the mountain.

This is what shelters always do: they remove burdens and reframe perspectives. When you're walking up a mountain beneath an unleashed sky, you may labor under the misapprehension that it is your job to hold up the heavens. But a few feet of primitive stone roof is more than adequate to liberate you from that notion.

Great philosophers and spiritual teachers have always known that *how* we see determines *what* we see. The story we tell ourselves is more powerful than the things that happen to us. I have a story, and you have a story, but the problem is that sometimes *the stories have us.* Your story can be your shelter or your prison.

Stories can trap us in deceptions about who we are and what we can expect, or stories can be shelters that allow breathing room for a spacious reinterpretation of our very selves. If fight, flee, and freeze were in fact the only three options in the face of fear, our story might appear to be a life sentence. Thankfully, each of us has access to a permanent pardon: the fourth way is an adventure in setting free the captive within.

I FIRST MET the poet, theologian, and philosopher John O'Donohue after a talk he gave about love as the only antidote to fear. John wove tales about the extraordinary permeating the ordinary, and his presentation left me considering how, in a culture that devotes more time to suspicion than to wonder, the most important task is to cultivate the capacity to love yourself first. Getting to know him, I discovered a distinguished intellect married to laughter so loud it could almost drown out the noise of airplanes, so warm it could help cast out the shadow of my deepest depression.

And then one day, the phone rang, and my life clicked onto a new axis.

John invited me to drive a minibus on his annual tour of the west of Ireland, an eleven-day existential extravaganza of pilgrims wandering across the Burren and the terrain of our own souls. We were based in a little village in County Clare, where the harbor imitates the womb-like welcome of the divine love to which John's work was a compelling invitation. I had known about this tour for a few years and had looked on with envy because I knew I could not afford the fee. But here I was, as I often am surprised to be, with an unexpected invitation to do the very thing I thought I would never get to do. It was an easy yes.

Prior to joining John's retreat, I may have been smart enough to know I was human, but I had not begun to appreciate the gravity of the status. It sometimes takes a companion more capable than me to teach me what I already know. Sometimes it takes imagining what someone wiser than me would do and then doing that. John was wiser than me.

By the time I met John, I was well versed in the theater of living from the shadow. I would addict myself to sugar or the internet, falling into a spiral of consuming fear or envy (which is its own kind of fear) that had me more concerned about the latest civil war or celebrity divorce than about my own health or about inhabiting courage or making beauty.

I would dive into cynicism, be magnetized by misplaced rage, consider the whole world my personal concern, fix my sights on others' wrongs, experience the empty catharsis of a Facebook comment smackdown—and in the end, do precisely nothing about the thing that had me worried in the first place. So great was the whelming of other people's suffering that their stories seeped through my highly permeable boundaries. I allowed the news media's overemphasis on the spectacularly broken to become, in John's words, "the mirror, enshrining the ugly as the normal standard," and I was often paralyzed by it. No good would come of the fact that I knew the death toll of whatever global crisis had been considered most worthy of tonight's headlines. I would delve into ugliness editorially controlled by people I did not know and might not trust if I did, and somehow I'd see only myself. I projected my shadow onto the stories told by media that, no matter how humane their employees wish to be, still compete to win the spoils of an economy devoted to fear and scarcity. I had bought the lie that I must always know the "news" or my life wouldn't be complete.

John would counter, saying that even those most alone and afraid and depressed can see—*need* to see—beauty. In fact, it is in the moments when we are most alone and afraid and depressed that we prove the efficacy of beauty as an antidote to death.

I would think, *It's all about me.* John would say, *Yes, but perhaps not in the way you think.* I wonder if this is what he was thinking at the crest of the mountain pass, before he made me an invitation I couldn't refuse: to step into a new story. A story that made me see the world with new eyes.

THE MOUNTAIN TRACK is called Mámean, in the Maamturk mountains of Connemara. The name means "Pass of the Birds," and historians say it has been a place of pilgrimage since the fifth century. Mámean rests near a settlement called Maam Cross, where there's a pub that in the telling of my friend Denis becomes the location for an elegant joke about René Descartes, a second pint of Guinness, and the limitations of believing your own thoughts. If you and I ever get to Maam together, I'll tell you that joke. Back then, we pilgrims were at the base of the mountain. We looked up. In the absence of helicopters or the *Star Trek* transporter machine, I invented what should have been an ancient Irish proverb: *The journey to the top of a mountain begins with a single "Sweet merciful God, are you serious?"*

God was, I think, and we were too, so off we set, traversing bumpy, pockmarked fields. This meant that every seven steps or so, someone would trip, and we would have to gather ourselves—rebalancing after a fall being one of the miracles available to humans and one of the lessons I learned on this magic mountain.

The first field ended when we hit water: a stream wide enough that it took some delicate navigation on foot. There were enough rocks in the water that a little game of stepping-stones was in order. John walked out to the middle of the stream and stood on a large stone, inviting us one by one to join him there, where he pronounced a blessing for the journey and lightly hit a shoulder to seal the deal. This was John at his most impish. Blessings, for him, were not words dusty and official—the kind spoken only formally and at occasions of utmost seriousness by men in robes. No, blessings were words of life to be spoken in the loving embodiment of what he called, in the title of one of his books, "the space between us." A real blessing becomes an act of creation, filling what was previously metaphysical emptiness as water reawakens a dry sponge.

So the blessings were spoken, and the shoulders lightly hit, and the pilgrims sent to the other side of the river. The metaphor of baptism—dying to an old way, being refreshed and cleansed, and rising again into a new life—was not accidental, nor was it ecclesiastically bound: everyone was welcome, and it didn't matter what your faith tradition was or whether you had one. The sole qualification to take this walk was an openness to light.

WHEN YOU ENTER into freedom, possibility comes to meet you, John would say. These are dangerous words when unmoored from accountability yet self-steadying, liberating ones when freedom matters more than money, status, or people-pleasing. When a river crossing has been accompanied by a wise Celtic priest's blessing to go forward, even a soul as uncertain as mine recognizes that it may indeed be time to enter into freedom.

So we bumped our way up the mountain. This retreat, full of all-too-rare things like holy laughter and communal silence, had been surprised also by unseasonably good weather. And when I say unseasonably, I mean it's *Ireland* we're talking about. We had been the delighted recipients of the hottest ten-day stretch I can remember. Every morning, the sun split the sky; the grass warmed up for an early yoga class. One of us lit the fire in the retreat cottage headquarters, but it was either out of habit or to invoke peak peat authenticity, as there was no need for its temperature-animating powers. By noon we would be walking, behatted, besunscreened, and beguiled by the landscape and the sky furnace that had decided to shine upon us. We got used to the Irish heat wave, so on the day we went to Mámean, we were expecting more of the same. When you enter into freedom, possibility comes to meet you, don't you know?

Today's freedom was wet. About halfway up the mountain, the sun suddenly disappeared behind the kind of gray clouds that, when they show up in movies, look like clichés. It became rapidly cold, a wind arising that appeared intent on making up for the time it had lost in the past week's more agreeable climate. And then the rain. Down sideways it came, like little darts, biting into the face. Glasses protected my eyes but soon fogged up. And the path became bumpier still, as we now had to watch where we put our feet lest a stray pothole invite one in.

The mind wanders in such times and places. In this time and this place, mine wandered to something wonderful. Meister Eckhart, the thirteenth-century German mystic, wrote that "the eye with which I see God is the same eye through which God sees me." There it is again: *how* you see determines *what* you see. You can be halfway up a mountain, for goodness' sake, and pay no heed to thoughts of the ancient or the miraculous or the beautiful. You can just be pissed off by the rain. The rain doesn't care, of course, and the rain on Mámean kept coming, relentlessly. And I was pissed off.

After what felt like several hours of stumbling up Mámean, we needed something to change. It was too cold, we said. Our faces felt like they were being hit by water being fired from a cannon, we said—a cannon hidden in a secret mountain cave, at the hands of an especially vicious strain of leprechaun.

The fact that we were now turning our minds to one of the most absurd stereotypes of Irishness was the final sign that something needed to change. We needed to stop. We needed a shelter.

THE SHELTER ON Mámean is actually a kind of chapel, built near one of St. Patrick's holy wells—places of pilgrimage, restoration, and justice, where the subterranean water not only was a metaphor for life but could help literally sustain it. There were times in Ireland's history when her people were not legally permitted to practice their religion—which, let's face it, is another way of saying that there were times in Ireland's history when the colonial authorities tried to stop her people from loving. Can't be done, of course, though a little dexterity may be required on the part of those being oppressed.

Holy wells sometimes became sites of political resistance, where folks would gather to reaffirm their community. They were also places where the work of inner healing could be marked, often by leaving a stone near the well as an emblem of a sorrow or a shame that the pilgrim wanted to leave behind. St. Patrick may have walked the Maamturk region, may have hung out around Mámean, may have even touched the well. Or maybe not, but it doesn't really matter.

And by *St. Patrick*, I mean the Patrick I choose, not the one who once a year gives Chicago an excuse to dye its river green, or anyone with a great-great-great-great-great-grandfather from the *auld sod* to wear oversized hats, or the entire population of redheaded America to get kissed by strangers. Patrick has unsurprisingly inspired narratives that would strain the credulity of even those who believe that My Little Ponies are real. Much of what people think they know about Patrick isn't true. There were no snakes. He didn't write anything about shamrocks. He wasn't even Irish.

But he did do something that warrants, at the very least, an annual parade, if not sainthood both religious and cultural. At a time when others saw us Irish as targets for pillage or indentured labor at best, Patrick was the first outsider to address us as *human beings*. Not primitives or backward or less-than. The primary point of Patrick, for me, is not so much that he converted Ireland to the Christian religion; it was that he considered us worthy to be loved in the first place. This stunning break with oppressive tradition is even more extraordinary when you hear the story that Patrick knew Ireland because he had been abducted and held captive there for six years. After escaping, he later returned to the very site of his own oppression to love the people there. Can we imagine it? What kind of story must Patrick have allowed to weave itself into healing him so that he could turn and face his fear—and not only that but show compassion to the place where he had been persecuted? To reject the prevailing story of Irish backwardness, of Irish nothingness, and replace it with Irish *holiness*? Is there a story in your life that could use Patrick's guidance?

WE WERE AT the top now. And there it was: near St Patrick's well, a stone altar on a stone platform with a stone arch forming a ceiling, enclosed on three sides, open at the front, its shape evoking the natural cave-like opening in the rocks to the left. Its aesthetic could remind onlookers of hobbits and magical swords and the fella who never actually kicked the snakes out of Ireland.

The rain still battered our faces. The wind still threatened to cast us back down the hill. Some folks took what they thought was a step forward but were lifted by their raincoat parachute a foot or two from where they had begun. But no one was going to turn around. We could see the shelter.

In ones and twos and clumps, we arrived at the gape; John ushered each in quickly. On other days, there would have been a priest behind the altar, and pilgrims would have to stand or sit on rocks in front. On days when the rain is like a plague of angry pine needles, no such ceremony is required. Forty-one of us squeezed in behind the stone table, against the stone walls, under the stone ceiling, planted on the stone floor. If we had not huddled before, we were expert huddlers now, human sardines canned on a Connemara mountain, sheltered from the rain.

And now stuck, sweaty, freezing. Alive, grateful—what next?

John spoke: "Gareth, will you tell us that story, the one about the Jack Daniel's distillery and the funny tour guide? It will warm us."

While we were no longer getting wet, there would be sore backs and tired feet to contend with tomorrow. But the privilege of concerning ourselves with such things had yet to contend with the most powerful substance human beings have been given.

The story.

Nothing can defeat a story. Once an idea takes hold, it can't be erased: you can only replace it with a stronger one. Hopefully a better one. So on the day when the first story was rain and cold and wind and fear, I unfolded a new story: about a droll tour guide in a whiskey distillery several thousand miles away, whom I had met a decade before and who told a tale about money and power and family and love and fermentation and security and sorrow and a lesson learned. It warmed us.

In the telling, the rain let up not one drop. In the telling, the wind howled as loud as before. In the telling, the thermometer did not move. But *it warmed us.*

THE IDEA CAME to me only after we had descended the mountain, after the retreat had ended, and after even John had died suddenly, his crossing occurring just seven months after our Mámeán endeavor. The wave of sadness would ebb and flow with the depth of gratitude for what I had learned from him. The earth of County Clare and the mountains and the sea boundary there have witnessed many a mystic search. We go on such journeys to forage for lessons that may not make sense until they are serving us later. After the intricate details of the memory of such a journey—a holy memory—have faded, sometimes a sheer benevolent force remains. And eventually that force may be given language. So not in a flash but over years of wrestling with fear, I finally understood that the metaphors we use for engaging fear are inadequate.

We speak of *battling* fear, or *struggling* with it, or *curing* it, or, as I have just done, *wrestling* with it. But shelters neither battle nor struggle nor cure nor wrestle. Shelters *shelter.*

When I arrived at Mámean, I was a person who wanted to work for peace, who was trying to love other people and make them laugh, but who on the inside was constantly living on the edge of debilitating fear. At the top of the mountain, I would begin to discover that the best thing I could do with fear is to build a shelter: a story shelter.

My story shelter would not make fear disappear. But in the shelter, I could learn something better than illusory magic, and I could decide to spend the rest of my life discovering it coming true.

Everything I've shared until now is in the service of showing that stories shape us and that we get to choose whether we write our lives as prisoners or as artists. In part 2, we'll look at seven of the most common fears and air them out, like that sandy beach towel. We'll give them a good shake, reorient them. Hopefully, we'll begin to see what's worth saving and what's best allowed to fade away into the breeze. We need not fear accidentally losing things we need, for when love is the protagonist, nothing true can ever be erased.

Don't take my word for it, though. You can test it in your own shelter, which is something that you partly discover and partly make, partly with others and partly by yourself. We'll talk about some instructions for shelter-discovery and shelter-making in the next chapters. Few things are more important, and here's why.

On Máméan, we hit fearful weather. But it did not kill us. We were sheltered. And in the shelter, I had the unusual experience of hearing my voice telling a story that evoked what can only be called *powerful* laughter—of the kind that bonds you not only to others but to yourself, breaking through the calcified boundaries of cynicism and hopelessness. That laughter was the laughter of those who, for a moment, are so overcome with the joy of seeing each other and being seen that they may briefly not be able to breathe. That laughter can break through and help you become the most powerful agent of healing your life will ever know: your own best friend.

It is the shelter of becoming your own best friend that will do for you what your fear is most afraid of. It is not a battle. It is an invitation to something new and perhaps even something that sounds antithetical to everything you've heard about how to deal with fear. Step into your own story shelter and begin learning a new way of being. Stop trying to fight fear.

For a shelter does not defeat the rain. And a shelter does not argue with the rain. And a shelter does not feel the need to argue with the rain, or battle with the rain, or overcome it.

It simply makes the rain irrelevant.

An Invitation to Name Your Fears

HERE'S A LITTLE exercise that can be done in half an hour. Try sitting still in a chair for ten minutes—or as long as it takes. Ask yourself, "What is it exactly that I'm afraid of?" Keep asking it until something like a satisfying answer comes. Write down or sketch your thoughts.

Put another chair in front of you and visualize the thing that's frightening you. Imagine this fear as if it were a person, describe them in detail, and perhaps even give them a name.

Step outside your usual pattern of relating to this fear. Imagine yourself to be their parent or teacher, perhaps even their friend. Remember this is not an actual person, just an imaginary personification of the fear. And you're not really their parent or teacher or friend; you are just imagining what it could be like to know that you have more power than this fear does. That you are bigger than the fear.

One of the Zen Buddhist koans teaches that beneath all violent anger, shame, and disconnection are fear and sadness. We rage, we humiliate (or feel humiliated), and we separate because we are afraid of losing something important to us or because we grieve the experience of having lost something in the past. Beneath this fear and sadness is deep caring—for the wellbeing of ourselves, our loved ones, and the world. But we often haven't learned how to express that caring without causing more suffering. We rage, we humiliate, and we separate because we don't know how to love.

So while thinking of the personified fear, allow yourself to imagine the wounds and fears that such a person might have experienced and that led them to be the scary presence they manifest for you. What might they fear losing or have already lost? What might they care about with which you could empathize? How might you hold healthy boundaries with them but also love them, help them, meet them where they are lonely? Again, write down or sketch what comes to you. Keep those notes or sketches handy as you continue this journey.

part 2

chapter 6

fear of being alone

I am what I am because of who
we all are.

—Leymah Gbowee*

NOT ALL WHO wander are lost, so they say, and most of the
time it's true. At the Tillysburn Roundabout in the winter of
1987, when I was twelve, it was not true.

The Tillysburn Roundabout lies at the intersection of my
hometown and the mouth of East Belfast. You can approach
from three directions: the small slip road from Strandtown,
the dual carriageway from Holywood, and the Sydenham By-
pass. It's been streamlined since I was a kid, but back then, it
really was a roundabout—one of those strange pieces of British-
Irish road system that Americans can't navigate. It was quite
brilliantly designed, connecting the three arterial routes above-
ground and containing an underground subway for cyclists and

---

* Gbowee was describing *ubuntu*, a concept of collectivity and mutual
  caring with roots in South Africa. The philosophy has been rendered in
  various ways and perhaps most popularized by Archbishop Desmond
  Tutu in *ubuntu* theology.

pedestrians, with three exits proceeding from the central circus. It was like one of those adaptors that connect more than one loudspeaker to the same hub.

It was probably the largest piece of structural engineering I knew before cease-fires gave way to the rapid gentrification, shopping mallification, and mirror-glass office blockification of the city.* Two or three times a week throughout my childhood, we drove in a car around Tillysburn, which provided the quickest route to city recreation or grandmotherly cake. But on the day my father asked me if I wanted to ride my bike into town, I was anxious.

On a bicycle, I would have to cycle down the hill from our house (exhilarating); then I'd have to pedal a couple of miles on the cycle path (tiring but necessary); and then there would be Tillysburn. However, after Tillysburn, there would be Nana, and chocolate, and Papa, and a pound coin folded into my palm. The bargain seemed unholy but worth it every time.

So Dad and I got on our bikes, went first down the hill, and then pushed our way up the road. About twenty minutes later, there it was: the Godzilla of road traffic control systems. In *Autobiography of Red*, the poet Anne Carson describes what a school building looks like to a timid child standing outside the "Main Door" that looms like the gate of hell, behind which is "a hundred thousand miles of thunder tunnels and indoor neon sky slammed open by giants." Tillysburn differed in that there was no neon, but there were tunnels—and if not giants, the fact that they lay underneath a road evoked in me a hitherto dormant fear of trolls. I didn't know much about trolls then, but I was certain they just had to be at the bottom of the hill.

---

* Belfast is yet lovely, and on the occasions when its decision-makers define a better place to live or visit based on what leads to human flourishing and the ecosystem to be well stewarded, it becomes lovelier still.

Dad zoomed into the underpass, flying down the ramp into . . . what? I had never been into the "under" of Tillysburn, so here comes the first fear: the unknown. I stopped at the top of the ramp, but the noise of the cars near me scared me enough to push me forward.

Dad was nowhere to be seen. I was speeding down the ramp into no-one's-land, and my protector had disappeared. Second fear: being lost.

Braking at the bottom of the ramp, I could see where I was. The hollow core of the roundabout, a concrete circle from which three exits proceeded. There were some grass and weeds growing from the breaks in the concrete, not enough to make it worthy of being called a jungle but sufficient to inspire the feeling that it had been here a very long time. Third fear: never getting out of here.

The three exits led to tunnels, which were unlit and of course reinforced the terror that was now tightening the skin on my face and searing my lower legs. It looked like I was inside a volcano, from which the only escape would be to run around in the kind of darkened cavern that Indiana Jones usually ends up in.

In my memory, the three access roads above me were overwhelmed with vehicles: hundreds of cars piling onto each other like a haunted house–monster truck rally mashup. In memory, it was a cold and gray day, wind nipping my bare arms and face. In reality, it was probably a day of average traffic, and I imagine the weather was fine too.

I did not know which way to go. I froze. All the guilt for things I'd done wrong or left undone seemed to surge through my body. I felt that I was nothing. I couldn't even find my way out of a roundabout. I was cold.

I started to cry.

This is what it feels like to be alone. Loneliness attracts the coldest kinds of fear. Indeed, loneliness may actually be an element in *all* fear: the fantasy of being entirely without support constituting one of the things necessary to make fear most effective in the first place.

The good news is that if you can learn to empathize with your own loneliness and fear of being alone, you can learn to dance better with all the other fears in your life. The blessing, as always, is inside the struggle. And those who have struggled with loneliness and the fear of being alone know something that others don't: the fear of being alone is not about the aloneness itself but the impact of the loneliness. What will we do when we are alone? What will we use to protect ourselves? Who will let us know that everything is OK—or help us get out of the way when it's not? Who will love us?

My father was on the other side of the roundabout, and I was scared. He might be angry with me for taking so long, the threat of which was now doubling my fear and making it even harder for me to think straight. I was weeping and felt ugly. I was so afraid that I could not move.

And this is the most insidious effect of the fear of being alone: it becomes a self-fulfilling prophecy. The fear becomes toxic, caking your body into immobility. We want to go on, but we feel that we can't. So we stand still, as if struck into clay like the poor people of Pompeii who didn't even know what hit them. Meanwhile, our lives become the thing we feared: lonely, and afraid, and afraid of being lonely, and more lonely still.

I am not lonely because I don't know what exit to take on the roundabout. I am lonely when I am overcome by the fear that there will be no one on the other side to receive me—no one who *knows* me. The fear of being alone can be like the fear of being invisible, that no one will ever notice me. That I will die as my most depressed moments try to convince me I have lived, unseen and unknown.

I ONCE WAS cared for by a wise therapist named Eolath. By the time I knew him, both his hair and beard were almost completely white (I call it the "trimmed Gandalf look"). He had a slightly asthmatic voice and a twinkle in his eye. The first time I sat in his warm room, I noticed a punching bag hanging from the ceiling behind him ("Some people need to hit something to get their anger out"); soft toys ("Some people like to cuddle them; others like to rip their heads off"); and phone books ("Some people need something bigger to rip"). He asked me, "So what does the critical voice in your head say when it's at its worst?"

I was stunned, because the critical voice in my head was not just a critical voice but a critical mass, and it had crowded out any space for the humility that would allow me to recognize that *other* people also have critical voices in their heads. Also, I hadn't known that therapists *know* we all have such voices in our heads and that inquiring into the nature of those voices is an obvious place for a therapist to start.

There was nothing special about my own critical voice, though I thought he was as twisted and powerful as Richard the Third (or at least the sound of Laurence Olivier's voice playing Shakespeare's menacing king). I responded, "It says, *Gareth, you're a failure. You're a loser. Your friends tolerate rather than accept you, you've betrayed God, and you're going to die young, most likely by your own hand.*"

Eolath scratched his mini-Gandalf beard and smiled. "Your critical voice is more articulate than mine," he said.

Stunned again. He had a critical voice too? What kind of therapist was this? On the one hand, he was being more open with me than any previous therapist. On the other, surely good therapists have conquered the critical voice. Was he really any good after all?

So I asked, "What does your critical voice say?"

"*Eolath, you're a sick, lazy f#!%.*"

I had not expected this. But it is what I needed. "When did you last hear it?" I asked.

"Oh, about 10:30 last night. I was going to bed, and my inner adult said, *Go and brush your teeth.* My inner child said, *No, I'm not f#!%ing going to brush my teeth,* and the critical voice said, *Eolath, you're a sick, lazy f#!%.*"

Eolath had struggled with fear earlier in his life, and he had even changed his name because of it. He had told a spiritual director about his fear that he was doomed to repeat the mistakes of his father. I don't know if his father's mistakes were dramatic or ordinary, but of course the radical rejection and healthy integration of parental projections are rites of passage offered to everyone, accepted by few. The spiritual director, who was an elderly nun, invited him to consider that there is more going on in the subterranean channels of the psyche than the influence of just one person. She suggested he meditate on a Gaelic word that can be understood to mean "wisdom of the fathers." This word conveys the idea that we are fathered—and mothered—by more than just our birth parents. Sure, there could be some awful shadows among our ancestors, but there will be saints in our lineage too. We can choose to nurture ourselves by leaning on and learning from the wisdom of the many fathers and mothers who have formed us. A Gaelic term that can convey this truth is *eolath*.

———————————

THE WISDOM OF the fathers and the mothers is that the healing of loneliness lies not in knowing which exit to take but in *being known.* "The essential religious experience is that you are being known through more than knowing anything in particular yourself," Richard Rohr writes. I think he may mean that true knowing is a two-way street between us and the divine (or higher power, or universe, or God, or whatever may be the best synonym for Love). The way to overcome the fear of being alone is to find friendship with God and with yourself.

At long last, of course, I escaped from the Tillysburn underpass; there were only four exits, so it was never going to be an endless struggle. Tillysburn has grown into something larger now. There's more traffic, and the roads have been widened, so it's best renamed an *exchange*, not a *roundabout*. Appropriately so, for what needs to happen with our loneliness is an exchange too: giving up one way of thinking for another. Not knowing the right exit to take on the roundabout is not the point. Knowing isn't as valuable or life-giving as being known. Being known is not something to be achieved but *experienced*. And it can be experienced right now through a practice that is often called prayer but is accessible to everyone, no matter your tradition or belief.

Many practices help lead us to the door of prayer: meditating, sitting still, being in nature or amid art, preparing and eating a meal from sustainable food sources, asking what is elevating or elating and opening yourself to it. Any practice that unfolds love to you can be considered prayer.

The United Church of Canada's "A New Creed" begins with these words: "We are not alone, we live in God's world." Prayer is therefore not a chore. Prayer is one way to *community*. Prayer literally *remembers* us into the experience of not being alone.

What will heal your loneliness is the journey toward becoming your own best friend. If it seems counterintuitive to suggest that the way to heal your loneliness is to spend more time alone with yourself, I understand. But plenty of healing comes from doing the opposite of what seems obvious. The mystics know that you should practice meditation an hour each day—unless you're too busy, in which case you should practice it for twice as long.

Another good practice is to write down a list of things you would do to show someone you truly loved them and a list of things you *wouldn't* do to someone you truly loved. I'm not talking about boxes of chocolates or favors, although of course they can be welcome tokens of affection. Here I mean things that go deeper: affirmation of the most profound truths, invitations to life-giving silence, permission to rest yourself in the mercy you would show someone else. Then choose to do one thing from the first list *for yourself* each day. Also let some of those first things include practices of kindness toward others. The answer to two questions—how you can be of service to your own loneliness and how you can be of service to the loneliness of the world— is the same. Become your own best friend, and you will become the kind of person to whom others flock. Your boundaries will become healthier, your sense of need will transform. And one day, you might look in the mirror and see the reflected glory of the sun.

THE FIRST WAY TO NOT BE AFRAID: BEFRIEND THE DEEPER YOU

I'VE COME TO believe that one of the things that we all need is for everyone to become their own best friend. People who love themselves well are not only totally wonderful to be around; they tend not to start any wars either. The people who love themselves are the ones who cultivate a relationship with what I've earlier called the core beneath the core—the true self—and live from that place.

The simplest and most powerful practice I know for befriending the true self is active meditation.

Sit straight in a comfortable chair, hands folded, eyes closed. Breathe slowly.

Repeat these words out loud:

> I am being made by love and for love.
> I am being made by love.
> I am being made.
> I am.

Continue to breathe slowly, not concerning yourself too much with the thoughts that seek to distract.

Do this for six minutes at the beginning of the day. Try it for a week. See what happens.

chapter 7

fear of having done something that can't be fixed

This is the world we live in.
A world where half the time
we're in denial and the other half
we're at war.

—Sam Wells

PAUL EDDINGTON, BORN in 1927, died in 1995, a Quaker
with an upper-crust English accent, a pacifist and conscientious
objector, and one of the most beloved actors on British television
in the 1970s and 1980s: Paul Eddington was not "cool" in any
sense that would lead to a magazine cover shoot. But when he
fell terminally ill, he revealed himself to be capable of an un-
common form of courage and deserving of serious attention. He
gave a final TV interview so painful in its honesty that it was
both difficult to watch and impossible to turn away. When asked
what he would like as an epitaph, he gave the kind of rare answer that deserves to be remembered:

"He did very little harm."

He did very little harm: these words may seem pessimistic.
Perhaps they evoke the false modesty of a celebrity seeking to

atone for a life poorly lived—or, at the very least, as a depressed lowering of expectations of what a human can be. But when I heard them spoken by Paul Eddington, his voice husking, his face burnt and crumbling from the cancer that was to take his life only a few days later, not only did they have the ring of truth, but I felt he was giving his listeners a gift that might just lead to a change of direction and a renewal of our hope that we could do better. It is all too easy to live unconscious of our impact and to go through life wreaking havoc in the lives of others. Indeed, some of the greatest pain is caused by those who believe, without wisdom or accountability, that they are doing good.

He did very little harm: I like the sentiment, and I respect the intent. And while active commitment to reduce harm is a good thing, making mistakes cannot be avoided. The more important question—and I imagine Paul Eddington might agree—is "What do we do with the knowledge of our own power to hurt and to heal?" There is wisdom in the idea that none of us can *make* anyone else feel something; it's more accurate to describe feelings being *stimulated* or *contributed to* rather than *caused by* another. It is liberating to keep this in mind when considering both the harm to which our actions may have contributed and the pain that has come our way. It is liberating to remember that we can choose our response, whether the situation invites us to make amends for the impact of our actions or to withhold revenge and move toward forgiveness for the wrongs done to us. Suffering is so often not the result of active malice on the part of enemies but simply arises because we don't take life seriously enough or because we downplay the enormous possibility manifested in just one human being. Or we take *ourselves* too seriously, acting as if the world revolved around us. Or we fall asleep at the wheel of our own conscience—not caring about our impact on the world or perhaps not believing that we could have any. All of us have been hurt, and all of us have contributed to hurt in others. We are neither angels nor demons—we are humans, made for and by love, and love will not force us to be good. It will simply show us through our own experience that we can choose either to enhance love and evolution or to stimulate pain and diminishment.

When we sit still long enough to listen to the deepest voice within, we know this is true both for our individual selves as well as for the communities and nations to which we belong, from whom we are excluded, or about which we hold mixed feelings. For centuries my homeland was immersed in a story of conflict that involved violence and religion. Our story of religion was divided not between Protestants and Catholics but between reactive puritanical imperialism and creative imagination toward the common good. One mistakenly and perhaps unconsciously tried to control both the people as a whole and the individual soul, and the other lived into the possibility that love might open more doors than it closes. And the line between repression and imagination does not necessarily divide one person from another but usually runs through each one of us, to a greater or lesser degree. The northern Irish civil conflict was not *about* religion, but it depended on *repressive* religion to define the ethnic boundaries. Our peace process was not *about* religion, but our story of conflict transformation would not have unfolded without people whose *creative* religion motivated them to make peace. We knew some of the heights and depths of which human beings are capable. We knew the immense suffering that results from people opting for violence as something other than a last resort or living as if aggression can repair things. We also heard echoes of the best religious traditions in the heroism of friends who risked their lives meeting with enemies to seek a just peace. Religion was shadow, and religion was light. It was, as they say, complicated.

In facing the complicated fact that religion can either imprison or liberate, can regress us or launch massive leaps forward into greater love, I have prayed, I have asked, I have sought, I have knocked at the door of heaven and pled my case before what may be either the listening ear of the divine or my own projected fantasy of God—or some combination of both. Sometimes I have felt as if I have received an answer. Sometimes I have felt only absence. Sometimes I have been so plagued by the question of what it is that leads human beings to attempt to destroy the light in each other that I have been paralyzed by fear. Sometimes I have seen beyond this fear into what seems like a bigger picture of hope. And I have wondered, if it is good enough for St. Francis, and for Gandhi, and for Dr. King, and for Dorothy Day, and for Desmond Tutu, and for countless other saints whose spirituality fuses with activism for a better world, then maybe it should be good enough for me.

At the end of it all, I am left with the soft memory of Paul Eddington's voice inviting an epitaph. And I ask, as I find myself in my midforties—an age by which I had expected not exactly to have solved the mystery of the universe but perhaps to understand a little more of what we're here for—what kind of life is worthy of Paul Eddington's epitaph? What would it mean to do "very little harm"? How can you find God when you've been damaged by bad religion? In a world in which fearing others is, for some of us, just common sense—in which a higher fence is a sign of home and suspicion is the way we're told we must relate to one another—how is it possible to enjoy your life without diminishing anyone else's?

A COUPLE OF days after he started college, my buddy Nate pulled his car into the driveway of his new apartment. It was late at night, so it was too dark for him to investigate the bump he heard on his way in. The next evening, he saw the car of the neighboring driveway with a significant dent on the side. He remembered the bump from the night before, and he realized the dent must be where his own car must have hit his neighbor's. The amygdalae switched on, the fear of eons descended, and Nate froze.

For eight whole weeks, he tried to avoid contact with the owner. He hid in his own home. Didn't invite the guy to the housewarming.

Crossed to the other side of the street whenever he saw him outside. Then one morning, the guy was at his door.

"Hi, there. Just wanted to introduce myself. I'm your neighbor."

Nate froze. Red faced, embarrassment and fear fully integrated with each other, Nate begged for forgiveness.

"For what?" asked his torturer.

"The car," Nate said. "It was me who dented it. When I moved in. I'm so sorry."

"That little dent? Don't be ridiculous. That happened two years ago. My name's Jim. Good to meet you. Wanna get a beer?"

SOME OF US feel incompetent most of the time; most of us feel this way some of the time. Some of us were formed in environments that shame us, and we learned to be at war with ourselves, overstating the harm we think we have done and ignorant of the places we might actually make amends. Many of us go through life with the fear that we have done something irreparable. We are caught in the memory of a circumstance that may have happened only once but recurs in the mind as if it were taking place right now.

In this very moment, I can call up the teenage memory of making a snide comment about someone who by accident overheard it; the twentysomething embarrassment of making a romantic step toward someone who turned me down; the more regular anxiety that I am completely alone with my fears. This is not true, of course, but it is *real*.

Northern Irish poet Paul Hutchinson writes of a man released from prison into the community that once honored but now scapegoats him. He attends therapy to heal his broken mind, but only more brokenness ensues. The chair he sits on won't hold his weight and collapses. As Paul writes it, "Counseling sessions failed when I broke the chair I sat on / In anger or aggression (I get these terms confused)."

You might identify. You may know that chair—and that weight—well.

There is a *personality* to these fears. You could say they are like darting yellow jackets, buzzing in the back of the head, threatening to sting the life out of even the happiest day. They have stolen my joy more times than I could count.

The fact that there are nasty little stingers there in the first place is, as we have seen from our discussion of Hobbes and Tigger and Tony, a pretty ancient and universal fact. We've all had the experience of feeling guilt and being too afraid to apologize for something, lest our shame overcome us. And we've all had the experience that when we finally *did* apologize, the person we thought we had wronged didn't care about, didn't notice, or actually welcomed what had happened.

The converse is true as well. We've all nursed wounds or borne grudges about things we just *knew* not only had taken place but were done with malicious forethought, despite the alleged offender being entirely unconscious of the offense. This little lie has the most power when we tell it about people we feel close to, for the wounds of a friend cut deep. Perhaps the deepest cuts come from friends who didn't even know they were cutting. The scenario is all too familiar: one friend feeling hurt by another, who doesn't even know, and the friends going their separate ways because neither is willing to let down their guard. We've all lost friends this way. We have probably all rejected friends this way too. When the bees buzz, sometimes it's us doing the stinging.

One of the marvelous things about human frailty is that the roots of the solutions to our most seemingly intractable problems are found *inside* them. Oppositional energy, says Richard Rohr, always re-creates itself. So fighting against our fear and anger and shame simply makes us feel more afraid, angry, and ashamed. If we slow down and think for ten minutes, we may find that the answer to our struggle is *within* the struggle.

Because it's not just our friends who have hurt us (or who think we have hurt them). We are hard enough on ourselves without needing to add anyone else into the mix. You likely subject the magnificent and beautiful person you are to even harsher judgment than that which you direct to people you might even consider your enemies. You have likely judged yourself worthy of public flogging more times than you can remember. You have made betraying your inner glory into a way of life. You have done this because our culture teaches us to see life through a myopic lens.

The antidote to the *fear* of having done something that can't be fixed is to accept the *fact* that you probably already have or that you will in the future. Forgive yourself. Not that you get a free pass for being a jerk (or worse). But even my friend Don, one of the saintliest humans I've known, grieved his divorce by saying, "I thought I'd get through this life without hurting anyone. I was naive."

But there's better news: just because something cannot be *fixed* does not mean its wounds cannot be *healed*. Again, the beautiful thing about human problems is that they contain their solutions. If I want to have better friends, I have an opportunity in this very moment to become a better friend to myself. If I fear having done something that can't be fixed, I might remember that my perception is a story I'm telling myself. This story doesn't fundamentally belong to me, although I may have loaned myself to it for so long that it thinks it owns me. The memory of the cigarillos in Paris reminds me always that, at an absolute minimum, we never know when a story is over, especially when we're in it. What feels like something that cannot be fixed today might be remembered very differently tomorrow.

That is the *minimum* we can assume to be true: that we never know when a story is over. And if you're struggling with your story today—either the one you tell yourself about how you've been hurt or the one about how you've hurt others—there are two ways to move from that place. You can keep telling the same story and live in the past (or the future). *Or* you can make what our brothers and sisters in twelve-step programs around the world call "living amends."

What does it mean to live amends? If you feel you've done the hurting and you are sure it would not add to the pain of the hurting person, gently ask if they would be willing to hear your apology and offer of amends. They get to decide. If you're not confident that you would not add to the pain by directly acknowledging the impact of your actions and offering amends, then live your amends in another way. If you feel you are the one who has been hurt, then do two things: Seek a friend who will listen to your pain with empathy and healthy boundaries (both their own boundaries and the ones they will help you hold), and in the meantime, show kindness to someone else today. Do it intentionally and in a way that interrupts the flow of your day. I promise you, what will happen will look like a miracle. Because the other wonderful thing about the solutions to human problems being contained within the problems is that kindness works like sound waves in a perfect acoustic chamber. Kindness shown to another bounces back into you, as if you were giving your inner glory the most magnificent smile.

PERHAPS YOU'RE THINKING, *That's easy for you to say.* I can, of course, only imagine your particular fear, just as you can only imagine mine. So for those of us who have come to believe that this fear—the terror of having done something that can't be fixed—is one we are simply doomed to live with, here's a little final note. Of course it may seem easier to diagnose a problem than to implement a solution. Those beautiful ones who are struggling daily with inner voices that seek to restrain, inhibit, assault, or curse are heroically giving themselves to the journey toward being more human. They are magnificent, and they deserve the kindest, most loving energy to support them.

At the same time, those who have indeed made terrible mistakes face an often lonely road toward restoration. The retributive element of our culture mitigates against such restoration, for both the people responsible for causing suffering and those who have survived. Don't get me wrong, there is a place for healthy lament and proportionate mourning of what we have done. But making appropriate amends is not the same thing as taking revenge on yourself. There is a task of discernment to be done to figure out the difference between a healthy conscience and narcissistic or masochistic delusion.

It is also important to learn to speak about forgiveness in ways that honor its complexity and the pain that stimulates the invitation to forgiveness in the first place. Much is spoken about forgiveness, little understood, and too often survivors of great violations may be shamed or even retraumatized by the pressure to embrace the person responsible for the violation or to deny the gravity of their impact. I prefer to see forgiveness as a continuum that begins even before the violation occurs, with a life of compassionate boundaries arising from a deepening acceptance that humans often "know not what we do." When a violation does occur, pain must be honored—not only is it the psychologically and spiritually healthy response, but to do otherwise would be to continue the violation. And with the pain will likely come an impulse to hurt the violator. The forgiveness journey continues when we choose to withhold revenge—and this is not the same as pretending there should be no accountability or that there is no need for amends. In situations where great violation has occurred, we need supportive community to surround us, to share the burden as best as is possible, to help us step back from the brink of either returning an eye for an eye or harming ourselves. Depending on the nature of the violation, withholding vengeance can be a heroic act. And if the survivor does nothing more than withhold revenge, they should be affirmed as being on the forgiveness journey, respected for their courage, and not pressured to do anything that would further violate their well-being. Such loving attention, such patience, such tender holding of those who have been violated can, of course, help create the conditions whereby further steps may be taken on the forgiveness continuum. A society fluent in forgiveness as a journey that cannot be coerced and in accountability as restraint and restoration not vengeance would be a society in which survivors would do more than merely survive, and even those responsible for the violations could be transformed for the better.

Forgiveness is not understood in the dominant culture as a gift that can release both perpetrator and victim—at least not yet, but there are hopeful signs. Perhaps an equally great gift is when each of us locates the place within that can empathize with even those responsible for the worst human behavior. This is not to justify their behavior but to participate in the process of both healing the past and nurturing a more whole future.

As with all fears, the fear of having done something irreparable diminishes in the face of acknowledgment that someone, somewhere, has the same fear. And in some sense, each of us has left an irreparable mark on the world, redolent with both light and shadow.

But we ourselves are never the best judges of how much light or shadow we have brought. That's what community is for.

Sharing your fears with other people committed to the journey of emotional maturity will almost *always* reduce those fears. The Golden Rule universally present in world religions and wisdom traditions teaches to do to others only what you would want them to do to you; of course, this also means to *not* do to others what you would not want them to do to you. We usually emphasize the part of this teaching that refers to the wounds enacted upon or received from someone else, but in so doing, we ignore the fact that following the Rule must begin with those daggers that point inward. We know we are supposed to be kind to others, but what about being kind to ourselves? The sharp voices—those that say there is no point moving forward because of something we did in the past—restrain us. The future is therefore cursed, so we live in self-punishing prisons of our own making. To add insult to injury, we may recognize that to live in a self-punishing prison requires a degree of narcissism. The narcissism that lies underneath much of our self-directed condemnation makes the fear of having done something that can't be fixed even more burdensome.

If that's where you are, here's some good news: First of all, narcissism itself requires a large inner psychic industry to keep it going. It eventually runs out of steam, and if you are the kind of person who seeks discernment in a healthy community, you'll probably be gently challenged by one of your beautiful cohorts before that happens. If you are, ask for feedback, and be gentle on yourself too. Once we're dealing with the narcissism part, we can turn to the notion that the fear of having done something irreparable is really fear that you can't be fixed yourself. And if you can't be fixed, you tell yourself, there is no point even *trying* to be useful in the world. But the root of this fear is *also* narcissism. The notion that you could really damage someone as much as you think you have depends on an inflated ego too.

The beginning of the cure for narcissism is the same as the beginning of the cure for all fear: be kind to someone. Having a sense of mission in life is fundamental to cutting through the temptations of ego on one side and apathy on the other. The universal mission of loving other people may be the best way to focus a sense of personal mission—that is, giving such love to yourself is both the goal *and* the process. The mantra for self-love could be as simple as stating there is nothing wrong with you; it is only *believing* that there was something wrong with you that leads you to behave in ways that perpetuate the pain.

When Paul Eddington hoped to do very little harm, he wasn't just talking about other people. What you may or may not have done matters, but it is less important than the fact that living amends can begin right now. And the first amends you are invited to make—the foundation of all other amends—are amends with yourself.

Kiwi writer Mike Riddell tells of how, on his conversion to Catholicism at forty-two years old, he had to go for his first confession. He and the parish priest spoke together, but not in the familiar dusky booth—they talked in the living room of the priest's house.

After telling the stories for which he sought absolution, Mike nervously awaited the priest's response. I don't know the exact words that came, but they went something like this: "Are you willing to follow the discipline of the church?" said the priest, no tone of warmth imbuing the question. "Yes," said Mike, though not without some inner reconsideration of this whole conversion thing. He was not expecting this.

"I'm going to instruct your penance now, Michael," the priest continued. "If you are to be obedient to the discipline of the church, and if your conversion is to be honest, you will do what I say."

Perhaps this wasn't a good idea, thought Mike, wondering if he would have been better staying a freelance theologian rather than a son of holy mother church.

"What is the most beautiful place you like to visit?" asked the priest.

"I like to walk my dog on the beach," Mike responded.

"How long do you usually spend there?"

"About twenty minutes."

"OK. Here is your penance. Go out into the world and breathe in its fullness—its beauty, its struggle, its amazing possibility. Then go to the beach. Bring a flask of coffee and a blanket. Find a quiet place to sit. Watch the waves, and the people, and the seagulls, and the sand. Stay there for two hours. Breathe. Give this gift to yourself. And receive the knowledge of your own forgiveness. All is well."

The Second Way to Not Be Afraid:
Be Generous with Yourself

WHAT GIFT COULD you give yourself if you really believed you were forgivable? What would it look like to stop taking revenge on yourself?

Rest with these questions for a while, and maybe write down some responses to them. Then make a plan to do something in the next week that mirrors Mike Riddell sitting on the beach.

Give yourself the gift of at least two hours doing something life-giving, restful, and alone.

Reflect on the words the priest told him: "Breathe. Give this gift to yourself. And receive the knowledge of your own forgiveness. All is well." If it's true that you can't truly love others without loving yourself, what are you waiting for?

chapter 8

fear of a meaningless life

I am fearfully and wonderfully made.

— The Psalms

I WAS LOOKING for reasons to stay. Well, actually, I was looking at my left hand, using its digits to count the reasons to stay. My hand had become a psychological abacus on which I could chart a journey of almost four years, helping nurture an organization aiming for the intersection of spirituality, justice, and art. I had drafted an email resigning from the leadership role I held. The abacus would help me decide whether or not to send it.

This job had been one of the privileges of my working life, and the festival we planned was something I had dreamed about happening but always doubted we would be able to pull off. Yet it had happened: thousands of people had come together for a new kind of creative, catalyzing, communitarian experience and together had created something more than the sum of its parts. There was dancing and fire breathing and liberation; there was egalitarian education where we flipped the tables and had public figures ask the audience the questions with which they themselves were wrestling. There was the mingling of spirits and ideas among Grammy winners and Oscar winners and *New York Times* best-selling authors and musicians who play brilliantly in tiny coffee shops and writers whose audience is limited to their immediate family. There was hope, and it was good.

After five of these gatherings, there emerged the kind of challenge that invariably arrives on the doorstep of nonprofit organizations. The magic of spiritual activists and creatives for the common good gathering in one place was one thing; paying for it was another. So decisions were made to change the structure of the organization—decisions with which I differed, to the point of forming the judgment that I could not work effectively within the new structures. I feared the dream was dying.

I took a lot of time to think and discuss and pray. I read books about managing change. I felt angry. I moped. I paid attention to the memory of someone I loved who told me of a time he needed to make a major life decision and how the key for him was to heed the wisdom of a mentor's injunction to *steady* himself. And so on.

I had the merest idea of what self-steadying might look like, and I figured that imitating it would be a step in the right direction. Someone reminded me of the value of sitting still and thinking for ten minutes. So I sat still and *thought*.

What were the reasons to stay?

Money. The first was easy: this was a job that paid well, better than any job I previously had held. Leaving would launch me into financial uncertainty. So not only would the luxuries I had learned to treat as normal be off the agenda, but I might not be able to pay the bills that actually do constitute necessities.

Reputation. A small group had helped build this community and event from just the kernel of an idea. Leaving, especially when it had just become successful, would be sure to raise questions and dent my ego. If I stayed, I could keep building this reputation and indulging in the fantasy of being special. If I left, people might not care.

Power and platform. The gathering was popular, and it was developing a national and international reputation. People who otherwise attract large appearance fees were showing up for free because they believed in what we were doing. We could get people on the phone who had been, earlier that day, at the White House or producing Elton John's new album. It turns out that they're just people too, but I could feel like I was part of the center of something that could be seen to be important. And once a year, I could stand on a stage and say whatever I wanted for a few minutes to a couple thousand people. If I left, I might not feel important anymore.

Letting people down. Of course, it wasn't just me alone that brought this together. A team of people had collaborated to turn the idea of a progressive spirituality festival into a tangible thing, and there were the folks who had drawn together the tributaries of the often disorganized groups of spiritual progressives until they culminated in the river of the festival. If I left, would I be letting down both the people who had employed me and the members of the team I was leading?

Fear of the future. Most of all, there was the uncertainty of what would happen next. Four years in any one job these days is a significant enough rarity as to be considered countercultural— and when it arrives in the midst of the working life of a freelancer, it may even be thought of as a miracle. There was financial security, there was a community that welcomed me and gave me roots, and there was a vision that could expand each year. I could do this job for the rest of my working life if I wanted. If I left, none of these things were guaranteed.

Five reasons to stay: money, reputation, power, not letting people down, security. Five reasons that I could count on the four fingers and thumb of my left hand.

I held my hand up to the light, framed against the window in the room where I write, and gazed out at the trees. It was October, and autumnal leaves were burning with color. There were the books on my desk, the ceiling fan, the printer in the corner, the terra-cotta pot on the window ledge, the storage boxes on the floor. And there were the five reasons on my left hand.

A voice inside me spoke. *Even if you don't quite believe it, let's experiment,* it said. *Act as if you don't need acclaim or reputation, money doesn't define you, the world doesn't revolve around you, and what's inside you matters more than what you think other people think of you. Act as if the meaning of your life comes from just being a person on the planet, a manifestation of the ecosystem in relationship with and responsible to other people whose lives are just as meaningful as yours. Act as if you're safe, beloved, and free.*

These words reminded me of things wiser people had said. Other words came flooding back—mantras that had sounded nice at the time but that had apparently also been doing quiet work on my soul.

I looked at my left hand and pondered the reasons, one at a time.

Financial security is an illusion.
Reputation matters less than being genuinely known.
Power corrupts, or at least it takes a lot of energy to hold on to.
*The codependency embodied by the fear of letting people down
    has never been part of the recipe for happiness.*
*Believing you need to be sure of what is going to happen next
    is also a sure way of knowing that you will never discover
    anything new.*

I had gotten on board with the vision for this event because I believed in connection. But all these five reasons combined, in this moment, to produce its opposite. There may have been nothing wrong with the event per se, and the folks who remained involved with it were lovely, but I was dispersed from my sense of meaning, my connection with it, and my feeling that it was the "right fit" with my life. I was unhappy, but the leaves were bright reds and golds.

So I pressed *Send*, resigned from the role, and looked at the trees. They were astonishing.

THE GIFTS OF the age—the reduction in violence, advances in understanding the body and human relationships, communication across millions of miles—outweigh its challenges. But the challenges are real. They must be contended with if we are to navigate our way to the discovery of a meaningful life. The dominant culture often ascribes high value to things that are actually broken or to things that can easily break us. Things like money and power. There is a constant tension between what the dominant culture and economic system value and what nourishes the soul.

Addiction to money contrasts with being content with enough and seeing time as more important than things.

Obsession with idealized beauty collides with learning to live satisfied and delighted with the body that you actually have.

Fame may create obstacles to true friendship and knowing who you are.

Public rewards like Oscars and Pulitzers are not a vital measure of what it is to do good work with integrity.

Conquering and consuming do not compare with the gift of opening to the other.

Meaning comes most from a sense of a connection to the whole: the community of human beings, the grace of the ecosystem that permits us to be here, the higher goals of vocation for the common good. When that connection is diminished, we may feel the emptiness of wondering if anything matters at all. Our current cultural competition risks pushing us to ever more dispersed lives. Meaningless comparisons with people whose lives are much more interesting than yours (how many followers or social media "friends" do *you* have?) nurture expectations that are both unrealistic and damaging. Of course, as we are learning, each of these obstacles to a truly meaningful life has within it the secret of its own disappearance. Addiction to money breeds people who never experience the satisfaction of closure. Maintaining idealized beauty requires an industrial infrastructure and depends on a person's willingness to pretend to be something they're not. Fame, likewise, does not lend itself to the shaping of an authentic person; celebrities have to choose whether they are going to invest their energy in fighting to keep their fame or to find themselves in spite of it.

Money, power, and reputation do not equate to the meaning—or the *meaningfulness*—of your life. If you lack money, power, or reputation, you might actually be facing fewer obstacles to meaning than those who have too much money, who don't know how to use power for the common good, or whose sense of selfhood is wrapped up in what others think of them.

Wherever you land on the money-power-reputation matrix, the answer to the fear of a meaningless life is to share your gifts with the world. In other words, as Babette in the film version of Isak Dinesen's *Babette's Feast* tells it, "A great artist is never poor." She doesn't just mean physical poverty of material goods but something deeper still. If you share your gifts with courage and creativity, no matter how small they may seem, whether or not you have letters after your name or money in the bank, you'll find meaning everywhere.

Meaning comes from connection and interdependency. Meaninglessness comes from individualism and dispersal. There are a million meaningful things about each of us. But because we live in a culture dominated by fallacies about violence and success alike, we inflate our fears and diminish our structure of meaning in comparison to others. We don't tend to stop and look at the leaves on and falling from the trees, copper in seven shades, stunned by the fact that we get to be in relationship with such majesty. We deny our own magnificence in pursuit of plastic faces and plastic cars, failing to apprehend the miracle inherent in the very ability to think about such things. We rush from what E. E. Cummings called the "blue true dream of sky" to get into whatever activity we have accepted as our economic lot. We bury ourselves in a freneticism that would confound our forebears, vainly chasing the dream of sitting still and enjoying peace—while all the time, peace and stillness are there waiting for us, ready for our visit.

Of all the sperm and ova among millions—billions!—that could have met, it was yours. Of all the floors and roofs in all the world, the one you're always on and under is the one that has you most. Perhaps even needs you. Your home is the good green earth and her people, beautiful and wise and broken. You have a gift for these people, this earth, and yourself.

THE BODY STIRS. A shift of toe, a tiny shudder of shoulder, a sigh, the crusty opening of eyes. Breathing. Opening. Aware. Adjusting. And then, the first and most important question anyone will face, ever: *Are you willing to wake up?* Every single morning, every single one of us hears the very same question: *Will you wake up?*

The response can be shaped by all kinds of things. The light in the room: if curtains are open and natural light admitted, the body may be more ready to wake than the mind. We are learning that the quality of sleep, the dreams we've had, and even the type of light we saw before closing our eyes affect how or whether we will want to get up in the morning. The temperature of the room may contain the greatest deterministic power. Cold has an amazing ability to reduce the human anticipation to greet the dawn. But whether we sleep cold or hot, read an iPad or a paperback, wake up naturally without an alarm or are blasted into the moment by an electronic sledgehammer, we will still be faced with the same question, every single morning.

At some point in our lives, we are all diverted into acedia: a kind of lethargy that can be confused with laziness but is really a spiritual depression. For some of us, first thing in the morning, it can be easy to think that this state of acedia is not temporary. For some of us, it is a superhuman exercise just to peep out from under the covers, because fear blankets us. Our culture has adopted pithy little sayings that underline the common assumption that days are hard: another day on the grind, all work and no play, no rest for the weary.

The internet has made it possible for us to connect with more people from a wider range of backgrounds and to learn or enjoy more things than any previous generation. It has also given us a lot more shiny objects for us to crave, inducing a sense of lack or envy. It has bombarded us with more stories to worry about and illustrated more ways to imagine something better. It has contributed to both a lack of cohesion within nations and a sense of interdependent connection across the planet. And at the very moment that the limits of our knowledge are so rapidly expanding, it is also difficult to discern what is true.

It is time to wake up.

Meaning will reveal itself as you discern your truest story in emotionally mature community and as you learn to own it. From that place, you are invited to both ask for what you need and share your gift.

To experience the gift of our own meaning most fully, we must take time and pay attention to discovering what that gift is. This is countercultural, for while we live in an age when being famous is ascribed a kind of magic power, the question of *famous unto what?* is rarely posed. While we may be encouraged to "be ourselves," we are not typically nurtured on the path of actually discovering who we are and what gifts we steward. So the understanding of what you are *here* for may not come naturally. The affably wise educationalist Ken Robinson said, "You create your life out of the talents you discover. Or not." It is tragic how many people settle for so little. For fear of failure or loss, we live lost, failed lives.

Yet the discovery of a life's meaning doesn't just *risk* failure; it probably *depends* on it—or at least on being willing to be wrong or on being willing to be thought by others as weird.

Standing outside the glass doors of a Belfast fish-and-chips shop late one night, I saw two young men cruelly insult an older couple waiting at the counter. One of the couple, a man, appeared to have some physical and mental differences, and the young men were making fun of him. The woman, who appeared to be his spouse, responded to the insults by pushing one of the young men. It was more of a humiliated, pained push than an aggressive one; it came from rage, but it was rage on the side of despair rather than dominance. The two guys squared off with her, snarling profanities and threatening her.

The dozens of diners in the restaurant kept their heads down, anxiously hoping that ignoring the situation would make it stop. The scent of further potential violence was in the air. And I instantly *knew,* with a rare clarity, what needed to happen. I needed to walk with purpose and authority right up to the people, stand between them, and start loudly singing Dolly Parton's "9 to 5."

I'm not kidding. In my mind, I envisaged the aggressors turning toward me and away from the older couple. I predicted the younger men would be confounded by the breaking of the tension, the container for their violence no longer fueled by being mirrored but, instead, perforated by a clown. A handful of other diners would get up from their seats to hover nearby, showing the young men that they were outnumbered. That we would not be passive bystanders. I imagined the older couple experiencing the solidarity of community.

I saw this all so quickly, in a flash of inspiration, and my body filled with light and courage. I took one step forward, about to run into the building.

Then I hesitated.

Froze.

Stopped.

I did not, in the end, go into the restaurant, sing my song, and transform the situation in whatever direction might have ensued. I withheld my gift. I did observe from a distance as a sinister quiet fell, accompanying more squaring off but no more active violence. I saw the staff person at the checkout gently hold the hand of the woman after she passed her the fish-and-chips. The couple safely left.

I don't know what would have happened had I stepped up. But I know that the primary reason I didn't was that I let my anxiety about what people would think of me overcome my concern for the two vulnerable people being targeted.

We don't know what to do with people bursting into song at their local office cubicle or fish-and-chips shop. Folks like that tend to be thought of as weird. We give them a wide berth. I once saw a man dancing on a Southern California street corner, making magnificent spins on his toes and stopping to wave at the commuter traffic. His dance was rhythmed by whatever glorious sounds were emanating from his oversized headphones. And he spun on, and waved on, and smiled on. And there's a reason we call a spin a *revolution*.

Because when this guy wakes up, he doesn't have to ask, *Is there any point in getting up today?* No. He *knows* his mission, and he lives it. And he doesn't care if anyone else thinks it's meaningful or not.

THE THIRD WAY TO NOT BE AFRAID:
ASK WHAT'S YOURS TO DO AND HOW TO DO IT

THERE ARE BILLIONS of choices on the way that leads to a meaningful life or a wasted one. A meaningful life is easily recognized: a meaningful life is one lived in purposeful service to the common good, inhabiting the kind of community that invites our unique gifts to flourish and helps us meet our needs. Sadly, many of us never discover what we're here for, never finding clarity about how we are made to serve and receive in community and where and among whom we will most thrive. It doesn't have to be this way.

Start by asking, What are the most meaningful things I know about myself? If you don't know—and if you do—ask also *what others say* is meaningful about you. If you don't know that—and if you do—ask yourself what kind of person you want to be *near*. And let's expand on an exercise we tried in chapter 3.

Get a piece of paper and draw a line down the middle. On the left, write down all the things that you imagine would be life-giving to the people you want to be near. On the right, write down all the things that you imagine would be death-dealing to them.

Then fold the piece of paper down the middle, with the left facing up. Pin it to a wall or a refrigerator or keep it in your bag so that you can remind yourself to try to do one thing on the list every week.

Then sit still and look: at the miracle of your body, at the view outside your window, at the contours of the face of someone you admire. Close your eyes, and let time become something other than your habitual expectation. Ask yourself this simple question: "How can I be of service?" Do this enough, and over time, your life's mission will come to you.

Want the fast track? Your mission is to heal yourself and others through being of service; honoring the ecosystem, your neighbor, and yourself; and devoting yourself to Love. You get to figure out what that looks like. And as you live into it, you will discover the meaning of who you are.

chapter 9

fear of not having enough

> At the center of our being is a . . .
> point or spark . . . like a pure dia-
> mond, blazing with the invisible
> light of heaven. It is in everybody,
> and if we could see it we would
> see these billions of points of light
> coming together in the face and
> blaze of a sun that would make
> all the darkness and cruelty of life
> vanish completely.
>
> —Thomas Merton

JOHANNESBURG. CAPE TOWN. Pretoria. Places I've thought about for as long as I can remember, imprinted through a couple of decades' exposure to the antiapartheid movement, or at least rock concerts that raised money for the antiapartheid movement. (It's important to clarify to ourselves the difference between thinking about a thing and doing something about it.) I was privileged to finally visit South Africa about a decade after Nelson Mandela was elected president and attend a festival of art and reconciliation at the University of Pretoria, where we reflected and celebrated the role of creativity in the peacebuilding process.

It was approaching Easter, and the festival began with Archbishop Desmond Tutu speaking about the hope that we could go beyond ourselves into a place that we do not know, because it is a better place than where we now live. Art can make us discontented about what is and help us imagine a better future. I thought about how difficult it must have seemed to him during what he called "the bad old days" to imagine that the system that held his society captive would ever run out of steam. He always smiles, always offers hope, always seems to love in the face of anger. I have heard it said that he sometimes used to scream himself to sleep in the dark light of the horror his people were suffering. His happiness, though, shines through in those amazing eyes and in the way he walks with dignity and talks with such kindness and authority. It's because he knows the people need a vision. And he knows that there is something deeper going on than the worst things that are happening at any given time.

We spent the rest of the week working and listening to practitioners and academics, watching films and plays, and of course listening to music and dancing. South Africa is one of the few places I've visited where the logic of movie musicals seems realistic: when I was there, some people really did just burst into public song and dance at the drop of a hat.

On Maundy Thursday, when alms are shared with the poor, the day before Good Friday, when the state execution of the spiritual activist known as Jesus of Nazareth is remembered, I decided to walk from my hostel to St. George's Cathedral for the evening Eucharist. The story goes that at the height of the apartheid era, Archbishop Tutu was preaching at a service in the cathedral when dozens of agents with the South African Security Police filed in and stood in the aisles, taking names and pictures. Tutu got down out of the pulpit and approached the agents, warmly welcoming them to the service. His words, paraphrased here, were prophetic: "You are so welcome here today. But I know you are here for the wrong reasons. You think you are in charge, but this struggle against injustice—we have already won it! We have won! Because truth is on our side. And in a few years' time you will not be able to deny our victory. So I invite you join us tonight so that you will feel less ashamed of yourselves in the future."

I was eager to visit the cathedral as a kind of source pilgrimage, hoping that it might reenergize me for the peace work I was involved with in my own land. I asked the friendly woman at the hostel reception if she could advise a route and if it was safe. She told me the simple directions and said, "You'll be completely safe; it's a main road."

Within three minutes of leaving the building, for the first time in my life, I was mugged.

A YOUNG GUY comes up to me at an intersection and asks for money. I give him the first coin I find in my pocket—five rand, or about twenty-five cents. He isn't happy, so he shows me the rusty industrial knife he has concealed in his right palm and says in the kind of quiet voice I have always associated with ghosts, "I don't want to stab you." I am glad that he doesn't want to stab me because I don't want him to stab me either.

But I also don't want this encounter to be a victory for violence or its threat. Embracing nonviolence, or even seeking to hold hands with it, does not mean running away from violence, and it certainly doesn't mean letting violence think it is in charge. I need to find a way out of this situation that allows my dignity—and my body—to remain intact.

And then it occurs to me: *Tell him you're going to church. Maybe, just maybe, that will make him think of a time when he was once a good boy in Sunday school. Maybe he'll remember*

that kind lady who taught him Bible stories. Maybe he'll re-
member that someone once told him that in the face of every
human being, there is a divine secret. Maybe he won't stab you.
Or maybe you're patronizing him.

I reach into my wallet, pull out a fifty-rand note, and hand
it to him, saying, "Look, mate, I'm late for church." He sees
that there are other notes in the wallet; he doesn't ask for them.
Maybe fifty rand is all he wants. Or maybe my comment about
church has transformed the interaction into one in which I engage him as a human being. Although he is a guy with a knife
and I am a stranger, maybe what matters most is that each of
us is a *person.*

Maybe none of what I am thinking is true. At any rate, I
am feeling good about myself as I walk down Long Street toward the cathedral. After a couple of minutes, my body starts
to shake, a delayed reaction to the anxiety caused by the guy
who didn't want to stab me.

Then another guy comes up to me and says, "Hello, my
friend." I keep walking. He says, "Hello, my friend." I slow
my pace. He *shouts,* "Hello, my friend!" I stop, and he stands
beside me. I notice that he's carrying a plastic bag. I can't see
what's in it, but he keeps reaching his hand in and out, jerking
back and forth. I start to walk again, and inevitably he follows.
"My *very* good friend," he says, and I begin to wonder if he really means it. But the rapid-fire hand movements, in and out
of the mysterious bag, leave me anxious. So I decide to pur-
sue the now time-honored nonviolent resistance tactic of telling
him that I'm going to church. A beatific grin crosses his face.
"I'm a Christian too!"

Well, if you'd only said *that* before, my very good friend. I'm
being mugged by a brother! Hallelujah! (I guess this could be
seen as a fascinating metaphor for what passes for public ethics:
you can employ people with low wages and in bad conditions
as long as you don't sleep with your neighbor; you can build

missiles for a living as long as you don't fiddle with your tax return; you can steal from strangers as long as you do it politely.)

I say, "Look, if I give you ten rand, will you leave me alone?" He says, "Why don't you make it twenty?"

Mugging by negotiation. I pay him, and we part. To store up some anxiety reserves for the *next* time something frightens me, I decide to take a taxi the rest of the way instead of walking. But the driver has some wily ways too: thirty rand for a three-minute ride.

And so I go to Maundy Thursday Eucharist at Cape Town Cathedral, where we celebrate the ministry of Jesus to the poor and the courage of the archbishop who used to preach justice there. And I think about the hundred-and-five rand I spent to get here.

I wanted to do something other than fight, flee, or freeze in response to the three guys who had variously threatened or taken advantage of me. But the anxiety I felt at having been mugged pulled back my desire to be inspired by Archbishop Tutu. Fear has such a powerful way of rendering your best desires and deepest hopes powerless. But as we know from the story of the man condemned to a night in a cell with a rope he thought was a poisonous snake, it can also be productive. The authorities, who on the occasion of the fake snake proved themselves wiser than authorities often are, had given him the opportunity for further liberation, for they were the kind of loving authority figures who know that there are some lessons we can only learn by difficult experience. So what was the gift of the mugging?

CONSIDER HOW THE postindustrial culture in which many of us live defines *enough* on the basis of externals, particularly physical property. It's so powerful a truism that it seems unquestionable: *enough* means what you have that I can see. Special attention is given to the *what* that conveys status: a house, a job, a family (equated to the nucleus of two partners and small people living together), more money than you need, things. Yet we all know that houses mean mortgages, which mean stress. Few of us are content with, never mind derive substantial spiritual nourishment from, our jobs (which we keep because we believe ourselves to be subject to the cycle that defines *enough* exclusively in monetary terms). Family as defined within the limits of suburbia is often the location of anxiety and a sense of not being known, and happiness does not seem to depend on having more money than you need.

John Steinbeck was right to say of the economic system, "Men made it. But men can't control it." *Enough* is never enough. When we define satisfaction based on what we derive from a system that we cannot, as individuals, shape, we will forever be reaching for something that cannot be touched. The biblical story of manna from heaven arriving fresh every morning, more than sufficient for everyone but going stale when hoarded, is instructive here. If *enough*—and I mean the kind of enough that is actually *enough*—might be understood as *true abundance*, then to find it, we have to look beyond the machinery of contemporary economics.

WHEN I WAS about fourteen years old, ten pounds was a lot of money, and my grandfather was a lot of man. He was seventy-six with a brown overcoat, shillelagh, and tweed cap, and his chin was grizzled because he didn't see anyone except us and the minister and so didn't need to shave every day. Always a pound coin in my hand when I left, always a story about something in the war. There was always the offer to go up to his room and take any book I wanted. He had Dietrich Bonhoeffer's *Letters and Papers from Prison*, Mohandas K. Gandhi's *Autobiography*, Hermann Hesse's *Siddhartha*, and about six

Reader's Digest Condensed Books. (I took Bonhoeffer, Gandhi, and two *Digests.*) There'd be snooker on the TV (until I was about ten years old, it was always in black and white, which is not ideal if you want to understand how snooker works) and gentle puff-suck, puff-suck, puff-suck sounds he'd make with one of his seven pipes. The smell was holy, and I miss it in the deepest way, which is to say that I can still taste it even as I'm typing these words, more than a quarter century after I was last in its presence.

In the summer of 1989, we went for a walk up the Belmont Road and passed Jewell's newsagents (where I had bought my first movie magazine) and the shoe seller who specialized in oversized feet (it's a café now; nearly every old thing in the Belfast of my childhood has become a café). We were walking to a park (which is an apartment building now). It was the strangest park I've seen—basically a slab of concrete in which were placed eight cement circles, which may or may not have been intended as stepping-stones, but that's how they were used. I don't know if the city council had once intended to turn this place into a real playground, with swings and slides and, you know, actual things to play on. By the time I was fourteen, I was no longer a stepping-stone jumper (thankfully, that magic resurfaced later), but the park marked the boundary of Papa's daily walk, so I knew that's where we would turn back. Little did we know, a miracle awaited.

Just before we reached the park, Papa stopped. He put his stick down to catch something, pointed at it, and said, "There you go; that's yours." It was a ten-pound note. Someone had dropped it, and there would be no way of ever finding out who. (And if you're the person who dropped a ten-pound note on the Belmont Road in August 1989, thank you. I'll buy you a pint. Or two.)

It was wild magic to find something so spectacular amid bleak concrete. It was wild magic to have a grandfather who

would find a tenner and catch it with his stick and not even consider keeping it for himself. It was wild magic to have ten quid
in my pocket. The wilder magic is that a quarter of a century
has passed, and I still feel it. I don't remember the paychecks
I got over the past few years, but I remember the ten-pound
note that Papa found out of nowhere and gave to me without
even the briefest thought of himself. I remember the tone in his
voice, which can't be captured on paper; I remember him smiling; I remember me bending over to pick it up and asking if he
was sure I could have it. I remember going on a school trip that
weekend and the delight of having money to spend and the joy
of sharing it with someone. It wasn't a lot of money, but it was a
lot of magic.

A mugging in South Africa and an afternoon with my
grandfather. Two stories, two walks, two bits of money ex-
changed on the street. Scarcity and abundance. The mugging
matters more if I believe in the myth of scarcity—that there is
never enough. If a guy thinks he needs money so much that he
goes around threatening people with a knife to get it, it may
well mean that he hasn't been initiated into an interdependent
community that invites him to ask for help. As with the shark
who only eats people because we have overfished the deep sea,
if we wait until the guy brings a knife to what could have been
a much easier conversation before we ask what to do about it,
we're limiting our options to the least bad reaction in a dangerous situation.

Better would be to reimagine society altogether, nurturing communities in which even the guy with the knife *and* the
guy whose forebears stole his ancestors' land can call a cease-
fire and start getting real about what it means to share what
we have. There's *always* enough; the question is whether or
not we can bring ourselves to ask for it. The walk with Papa is
a lovely tale to begin with, but seen through the lens of the story
that there is *always* more than enough, it's the kind of thing

that happens every day. If we just learn the wisdom of looking in the truest places, asking the truest questions, and don't go it alone, we'll see that it's happening to us too. Trying to hold on to what we have always leads to scarcity, but sharing always generates more abundance.

THE MAASAI PEOPLE of southern Kenya and northern Tanzania are often considered to be an archetype of happiness; when the image you're most known for in the West is literally jumping in the air, that's no surprise. While the Maasai jump is actually part of a serious ritual of initiation into adulthood, and the Western interpretation that projects this as joyful exuberance may be misleading and even condescending, it is nonetheless apparently true that the Maasai are pretty happy. As Ed Diener, the psychologist best known for researching happiness, says, "The Maasai of Africa have virtually no cash income—they have their cattle. But the Maasai can meet most of their basic needs, and they are not exposed to western media. In contrast, homeless people in California—who often have much greater income than the Maasai—are on average not nearly as happy. They do not possess what others around them have, and it requires much greater income to meet basic needs in their society."

I would argue that meeting needs can be addressed more securely by expanding our circles of interdependent relationships rather than relying on greater personal income, but Diener makes an important point: the Maasai can meet most of their basic needs, and they are not exposed to Western media. It can't be more obvious than that, can it? I think we all know that there is something unhealthy about the way many of us consume media—or perhaps, more accurately, are consumed by it. I'm looking out my office window at the exquisite copper-kaleidoscope leaves of a fall tree, and there is no mediator between them and me. We're in relationship, and nothing is separating us or telling us what to feel or where we need to be. The role of mass media as "mediator" is worthy of sustained interrogation if we are to find a way to live amid the noise.

Ironically, it was James Bond who helped me understand this. Who better to do that, I suppose, than the twentieth century's most indelible archetype of conscience-free living?

Ever hear of George Lazenby? Most people haven't. But for a year or two in the late 1960s, he was something like the most famous man in the world. After Sean Connery decided to hang up his Walther PPK and abandon 007 (the first of three times he did that), the cultural mavens who owned the rights to the James Bond character hired an Australian bodybuilder and model to take the reins. Lazenby got to play Bond in *On Her Majesty's Secret Service*, which turned out to be one of the few Bond films that actually passes muster as a pretty good film in its own right. Lazenby's first line in the movie, after dispatching a handful of henchmen in a beach-based skirmish, is "This never happened to the other fella." Lazenby made the same true in his off-screen life.

After hundreds of interviews, photo shoots, and red-carpet gauntlet walks, he took a year and a half off to sail around the world. His manager had advised him that the hippie, radical 1970s would not look kindly on the suave psychopathy of a spy doing "the Man's" business, and this gave Lazenby the justification he needed to do what he already wanted to: get out of the Bond game.

That's why you probably haven't heard of him. For a year, he was king of the world; his later acting career did not turn out the way he had expected. But when I interviewed him for a radio program, he said he had no regrets at all, for if he had stayed James Bond, he would never have found the life he has. If he had stayed James Bond, *he would never have gotten to be himself.* Indeed, he realized that he had never really wanted to be an actor in the first place—it was the fake life of girls and guns and exotic travel and getting to kill bad guys with impunity that had appealed to him. He got to do that once. Why would he ever want to do it again?

THERE ARE COMMON elements to Papa's ten-pound note, Maasai levels of happiness, and the man who quit James Bond.

> *Authenticity.* Papa did not try to hide the money from me, and he knew it would be a richer choice to give the money away. The Maasai aren't pretending to be anything other than Maasai, and when their life-giving interpretations of reality are honored, things are well. George Lazenby knows the difference between a fake life and a real one.
>
> *Community.* When Papa gave me the ten-pound note, he fastened an even more unbreakable bond than had previously existed between us. I am sure I will remember this story for the rest of my life, and the truth of my grandfather's love is with me always, even though he's been dead for more than two decades. The Maasai's happiness is connected to their community bonds, their rituals for growth and the expression of need, and a sense of security among the people. George Lazenby knows that his joy is wrapped up in his experience of relationship with other people.
>
> *Time.* When Papa gave me the ten-pound note instead of keeping it for himself, he was buying an experience for himself: the experience of the joy that comes from making someone else smile. It was certainly a treat and definitely an investment in someone else, and he was paying now by giving it away, but I think he "consumed" the experience later, probably several times over. This experience bought us both time then, and it still buys me time now. When it happened and for years afterward—and now even today—Papa and I

actually owned time. The Maasai steward their world as a dance with the ecosystem, not a battle to conquer the land. George Lazenby walked away from untold riches and fame but bought himself time. For almost half a century now, he has tried to own his story.

Scholars Elizabeth Dunn and Michael Norton suggest in their book *Happy Money* five principles of the relationship between consumption and contentment: (1) buy experiences; (2) make it a treat; (3) buy time; (4) pay now, consume later; (5) invest in others. These are immensely powerful ways to think about how to relate to money, but there's an even more liberating truth to be discovered. For if you participate in authentic community that honors time, the notion of how much money you personally "have" in the bank will start to matter less.

Authenticity, community, and time are all about *connection*: to integrity, to the world, to the kind of breathing that heals our insanity. For me, the definition of abundance is the opportunity to step into authenticity (telling your own story), community (sharing your gifts and asking for what you need), and handling time with love (moving beyond worry about tomorrow and into honoring the hours you have today). Not having enough, in this light, has very little to do with either "private" money or property.

"BEFORE YOU CAN fight, you have to know what you are fighting for": author and activist Naomi Klein attributes this injunction to Aboriginal leaders who insisted she be immersed for days in cultural experience before beginning activist strategy sessions. She needed to know the land and the people and the music they made before she could be ready to take up the work of challenging government-industrial encroachment.

But such wisdom is not only applicable to the lofty goals of societal transformation; it's true also of the experience of simply living. The rules of our economy have created a conveyor-belt system dedicated to unchilding the innocent, a vision of life as a ladder whose rungs are defined by bank balances, power over others being valued more highly than power over yourself, and the things that make for love seen as aftereffects of economic achievement rather than ends in themselves.

Following the rules of our economy without thinking is like entering a pugilist's ring and letting yourself be pummeled without ever asking why. Our dominant cultural values dictate that we should be fighting to be rich or famous and that contentment and money go hand in hand. They're wrong. I'm suggesting that the most precious resource is not money or recognition and that indeed each of these tends to corrode. The most precious resource is, in fact, time.

What do we do with time? Do we let it control us? How can we learn to work with time? Can we learn to live from the place within that knows its own power to be guided by love? Oscar Wilde said that repentance can change even the past, and I think he meant that turning away from an old pattern can grant a new perspective on life and can make the old struggles worth it.

The dominant culture may ask, Who are we to think we can live differently than others? Who are we to think we can override the rules of endless industrial growth, to sit still and enjoy love more than cash? We may respond by asking, Who does the culture think it is to stop us? What does it think we are, machines? Who are we to suppress a revolution of kindness and sanity that will create a world in which time is our friend?

LET'S GO TO Cuba. Havana's streets, like those of New York or Paris or Jerusalem, are mythically alive with color and noise.

Unlike New York or Paris or Jerusalem, when you're walking
on a Havana street, you will sometimes see a man shaving. He's
looking into a mirror on a gable wall and wearing a tank-top un-
dershirt, the buttons on his overshirt undone, a kind of paradoxical modesty colliding with the somewhat naked self-expression
of doing his ablutions in public. In Cuba, or Mozambique, or
Iceland, you'll see people doing things that the dominant tech-
nocratic cultures have insisted we hide. Things like shaving on
the street or dancing bare-chested in the market or jumping un-
dressed into an ice pool, unashamed.

You don't see people shaving on the streets of Belfast, or if
you do, you might think they're not well. Shaving in Belfast or
New York or Paris or Jerusalem is a commercial endeavor par
excellence. Go to the aisles of any supermarket, and it's easy to
be overwhelmed by the range of products available to convince
you that facial grooming requires more than a simple piece of
sharpened steel and a bit of soap. And what we do with that
range is very strange: we spend billions of dollars on something we hide from everyone else. Yet walk down the street
in Cuba, and there is a man shaving. He'll be going about his
day, not concerned with what others think of him. The reasons
may be many, but they are certainly connected to one simple
fact that distinguishes Cuba from the dominant cultures: no
advertising.

We ascribe so much significance to the act of tidying up
the face that one of the largest corporations on earth brands its
products as "the best a man can get." The slogan suggests that
happiness or love or community or spiritual contentment is either impossible to achieve or not as valuable as the process by
which you trim the hair on your chin, in vain hopes of looking
like whichever soccer or tennis star happens to be advertising his
look these days. But in Cuba there's no advertising, so there are
no billboards, which means there are no public mirrors reflecting
idealized notions of beauty and success.

If meaning has to do with connection, and if connection has to do with authenticity, and if shame is the fear that we might lose our connection because what gave us meaning is under threat, then the intention of advertising is very simple: it reflects a totally unrealistic picture of what we can look like in everyday life, presents goods and services as if they were gods and salvations, and tries to make us feel the lack as if it represented our very lives.

The old story about the fisherman and the venture capitalist comes to mind. The fisherman is content providing for his family; he's on the boat one or two days a week and loving his community, learning, and dancing the rest of the time. His neighbors do the same thing, and everybody shares what they have.

The venture capitalist arrives, and he wants to take things to the next level. He wants to invest in infrastructure so that the fisherman can grow his business, take over the villages down the coast, and hire lots of other people to fish too. When the fisherman asks the investor what would be the point, the response is predictable.

"In about thirty years, you could retire," the capitalist says.

"What would I do then?" asks the fisherman.

"Then you could enjoy your boat, maybe only go out a couple of days a week, and the rest of the time, you could enjoy your community, learn, and dance."

WHAT WE CALL "the economy" isn't, really. As commonly understood, banks and treasuries rule things, labor and land are to be exploited, capital and money are both the generators of activity and the point. But this matrix does not remotely encompass the myriad sacred ways in which humans interact, share, and transact. For one thing, we know that what is often termed *domestic work* has been omitted from conventional definitions of economic activity, and there is also the vast range of things that humans do in the spirit of gift. The economy in which I live includes people doing things for no reward but the doing of it; or paying it forward and sharing money, tasks, and meaningful objects; or opting in to an alternative economy of gift exchange. In this economy, "goods and services" may deserve their names. The conventional economy thrives (or falls) based on the myth of scarcity. All my fears about not having enough are shaped by this myth. Famously, when John D. Rockefeller's net worth was about 1 percent of the entire US "economy," he responded to the question of how much money would be enough by saying, "Just a little bit more." You don't have to be Rockefeller to be ruled by the myth of scarcity, no matter how much money there is in the bank relative to your needs. The only way to be released from the myth of scarcity is to defect to the economy of interdependent gift. This doesn't necessarily mean liquidating stocks and throwing a party instead or living off the grid (though it might); it means consciously choosing to replace the myth of scarcity with a life story of abundance. And in this case, the best way to tell a better story is to live it.

Our fisherman knows the things that make for love; our venture capitalist thinks he can't have these things until he's nearly dead. Let's hear it for the fisherman—although let's not condemn the venture capitalist. The best way to overcome something bad is to do something better. It's good to face the things that don't work. It's better to repair them by doing something in their place that does work. It's good to note our inadequacies, our vulnerabilities, our mistakes. It's better to learn from them and risk the process of making amends. As best friends with ourselves, we can lovingly look within and see where we already have enough. The answer to scarcity is generosity.

It is said that children in World War II refugee camps had difficulty sleeping because they feared they would wake up hungry and homeless again. Someone with wise spiritual discernment decided to give them each a piece of bread to sleep with. The bread became a symbol of the reassurance that there would still be food in the morning—that they had enough today and would have enough tomorrow.

For years I was focused on my sense of lack: what I didn't have, what kept me feeling incomplete. I too lived from my shadow, not my medicine. I was so desperate to keep some things as "mine" that I even held on to my shame for dear life; at least that's something I could feel like I owned. What I stumbled into was how the simple grace of practicing gratitude for what is already more than enough can open this part of the heart. What I learned is that you don't have to heal all your brokenness before you start.

This is how it works, humans being on a spinning planet together. This is how we do it. We notice what we have. We figure out how to share it. We notice what we need. We figure out how to ask for it. We say thank you. And we cocreate miracles. One step at a time.

The Fourth Way to Not Be Afraid:
Be Generous with Someone Else

THE ANSWER TO scarcity is generosity. We'll share a practice in chapter 11 that helps us multiply generosity through weaving interdependent connections with others, sharing burdens, blessings, responsibilities, and even material needs. For now, here is a short practice to do on your own, stepping into generosity toward yourself and others and experiencing the abundance that is already here.

Claim an hour to do nothing. Make it an act of resistance to how the myth of scarcity demands absolute loyalty, down to the way we use every last second. Be generous to yourself. Receive the gift of time.

After half an hour, look up from your life, and in your mind's eye, quietly notice the face of the person who needs a letter from you.

Write it. No more than two sides of a page. But make it a real page of real paper, written with a real pen.

Send it. Love them.

Do something like this once a week. And you will know that there is always enough.

chapter 10

fear that you'll be broken forever

Children must be taught how to
think, not what to think.

—Margaret Mead

IT WAS THE summer of 1985—you know, *The Goonies*, *Back
to the Future*, and the longest nights I've known. I was ten, and
they were fifteen, and while I haven't seen them for over a quarter
of a century now, our destinies were tied together in ways I never
understood until after I started writing this book.

There's no need to name them because we don't deserve to
have the mistakes we made as children haunt us as adults. Living amends may be the price we are invited to pay and the gift
we can receive, but we can't make that decision for anyone but
ourselves. When our vulnerability is violated, we may experience repeated cycles of activated trauma; the legacy can overtake us until we begin to rewrite the story. The fear that we
might be broken forever loses some of its power when we accept
that one of the universal facts of being human is to experience
wounds that not only scar but terrify, and we may each have
contributed to significant wounds in others. But we can all heal.

What happened that day in 1985 was archetypal. It was in the realm of myth or Greek tragedy—which doesn't make me special, because something like this probably happened to you too. We just usually don't know how to interpret it: to see it for what it really is and to transform it into something good. One key to that transformation is that if we interpreted the original wound in mythic terms, the healing will need myth too.

They were a little local gang of aggressors, and I was one of the local nerds. When I saw them coming, it meant danger. They would ride around as a crew on their BMX bikes, and I'd hide. The leader hit me in the face once, for reasons utterly unfathomable. I couldn't have done anything that prompted it. I was just a kid. I was just standing there. I didn't have the power to do anything that warranted a defensive slap on his part. This was pure violence, out of nowhere, just to show his mates that he could do it. He was the alpha male, I was the prey, and prehistoric modes of being were still working in the bully's favor.

I share this story not for the sake of sympathy, nor to stir up fear, and certainly not to provoke the traumatic memories of any of you precious souls who are reading. So let me say this: there's a happy ending. And I'm willing to bet there's one for you too—and for all of us. The story of permanent powerlessness, perpetual violation, eternal victimhood, and open wounds is a kind of entrapment. It puts us into a cycle of returning to and fleeing from a terrifying thing that happened but that we find so compelling. To be free from the cycle, we must rewrite the story. And we can.

I DON'T REMEMBER all the details, and I may have some of the chronology wrong, but in short, at some point, I ended up tied to a tree. I was so lonely that I think I consented to being tied up, just because it meant I got to participate in something with others. Sometimes we participate in our own bullying because we haven't learned other ways to feel or how to simply ask for what we really want. This paradox is not unique to childhood.

They were threatening me. It was a penknife, but when you're ten and surrounded, size doesn't matter. "Say you're gay," they snarled.

I didn't know what *gay* was, other than the vague thought that it had something to do with men. And somewhere unreachable, I knew that it had something to do with me. I didn't have any conscious sense of attraction to anyone yet, neither boys nor girls. But there was, even then, something deeper and unarticulated within me that said I was different and that *this* kind of different might actually be *my* kind of different. Of course, that thought terrified me, although not as much as the teenager with the gang and the knife.

However, along with being terrified, there was also a paradoxical exhilaration—that is, I felt so lonely back then that *any* attention was welcome, even if it was on pain of homophobic stabbing. Eventually, in a mix of fear and hope for more attention, I said it: "OK, OK, OK, I'm gay!"

In a moment that would seem unrealistic in a fictionalized version of this story—but I promise, this actually happened—a man living near the tree opened his second-floor window and shouted at the bully and the crew to leave me alone. To unbind me and set me free.

In the irrational scheme of things, we all then went and played hide-and-seek together. It was during this game that one of the older boys aggressively coerced me to do something sexually that I did not want to do.

More terror.

Profound confusion.

The trauma that entered me that day took me into the bleakest and most grief stricken of places. For decades, at the far reaches of those places, there was a door. And on the other side of the door was treasure.

We all have a secret place that we fear to reveal. For many of us, this place becomes the laboratory in which we experiment with self-rejection. We fear that our brokenness is permanent. That we will never be able to reconcile ourselves with ourselves. Such a story often arises from a moment such as the one I have just described; it can also come from a series of repeated events. A story emerges that says we are somehow responsible for the pain we have experienced at the hands of others or that there is something wrong with us because we don't fit in. Such a story can become a wound even greater than the original one. When this story is not met with adequate empathy, trauma ensues. Your fear of permanent brokenness may not be the same as mine. But there are universal resonances we can all recognize in both the wounding and the healing.

I CAN'T REMEMBER a time as a child when I didn't think guys and girls were all gorgeous. And in adulthood, the entire gender spectrum seems to me a field of extraordinarily variant flora: chrysanthemums, mosses, radishes, asparagus, ivies, carnations, strawberries, mahogany, algae, and daffodils. My friend Mark once wondered, while musing on those poor benighted souls who are either gay or straight (as a term of amused endearment, he called them "monosexuals"), how it could be possible to love trees but not rivers, Montgomery Clift but not Elizabeth Taylor. For me, it was Michael J. Fox and Demi Moore. Both lovely, both inaccessible.

Clearly some of us are just made this way, or perhaps we are made, simply, with the *potential* to open ourselves to loving a bit more widely. At any rate, being enamored of, trusting in the beauty of, and championing the graces of the entire spectrum of gender are, for me, nothing more than the way it has always been.

It was the church and the culture, afraid of freedom, that told me no. When I was ten, and sixteen, and twenty-three, I knew no alternative. The only time I heard the word *gay* was in the context of sin, sickness, or—due to the particular eccentricities of my own church—demons. I didn't hear another human being say that men loving men was a good thing until I was twenty years old. I didn't meet an openly gay person until I was twenty-five. I didn't read a book or hear a talk that told me men being attracted to men was not only a fact of nature but something blessed by Love. I didn't know for sure that some men love across the gender spectrum—I didn't even know there *was* a gender spectrum—until I was thirty-five.

Along the way, there were exorcisms, including one from a kind man who told me that he didn't want to hurt my feelings but that after delivering me from the demons of lust and low self-esteem, he really felt there was one more we needed to get. "Is it homosexuality?" I whispered, desperate to be accepted but not comprehending that I was being invited to amputate myself. "Yes," he whispered back.

There were seminars and books that theorized about how same-sex desire is a pathological reaction to being sexually violated as a child or (in men) to having an absent or aggressive father. The facts—that most survivors of sexual abuse, like most humans generally, are heterosexual and that most people whose fathers are sometimes absent or aggressive are heterosexual too—were somehow invisible to the seminar leaders and book authors. When you're trying to use science to bolster prejudice rooted in a misinterpretation of a decontextualized two-thousand-year-old book, partly because you're scared that God might kill you if you believe the wrong things—well, you might want to reconsider your starting point. And yet I believed them.

There was also counseling—from another kind person, who taught me some good boundaries where codependency was concerned but still ultimately asserted that I was pathologically poisoned and that my ache to be simply held was a work of

Satan. There were years of self-imposed celibacy, for if I was indeed poisoned, I was surely also *poisonous*, and so I had better not poison anyone else.

And then there was a spontaneous weekend of love with a beautiful man, my self-directed homophobia being overcome by his openness and our connection. It's a long time ago now, but still the memory fills my senses: the fearful tenderness of an arm around the shoulder becoming a gentle stroking of the cheek, the moving of thighs closer on the sofa, the terror of wanting to nuzzle my face against his, the realization that we were kissing before we really knew it, the warmth of bodies given to each other, opening hearts, holding love, listening, breathing together, safety. And fear. For amid the ecstasy of being held by one who didn't shame me and who was strong enough to carry me and vulnerable enough to be carried, there was the voice inside that said God would kill me.

Your attraction to men is sinful, the voice said. *God is ashamed of you. You are also attracted to women. There is definitely something wrong with you. You can never truly talk about this. You will have to hide it for the rest of your life.*

So immediately after that weekend ended, I went straight to my pastor and confessed. I spiraled into the mouth of a tunnel of despair and for a good twelve months was weighed low by what I called *guilt* but was really self-rejection. What I called *repentance* was really a desperate attempt to retain belonging in a community that, despite being full of lovely people trying to be good, had boundaries that depended on denying my humanity. Telling me that love was sin. That tenderness was poison. That a bit of warmth with another person, on a cold night, was enough to get me possessed by a demon or eternally torn apart.

There's a cliché in some Christian circles that says God won't let you be tested beyond what you can bear. I have found this comforting at times. But really, when you look at it, it can't mean what folks intend it to. It clearly can't mean that your suffering will never kill you because plenty of people die in ways they would not have chosen. I think what it might mean in most circumstances is that there is a part of each human soul that cannot be destroyed. Most of us may be out of touch with this part, and the good news is that we can cultivate practices, habits, and relationships that open the channel. This, I think, is how Etty Hillesum and Viktor Frankl faced the Holocaust; indeed, it might be how both of them *survived* it, despite the fact that Etty was murdered and that Viktor's wife, father, mother, and brother were killed too. They knew, or discovered along the way, that there is a diamantine core to the human soul, unshakeable by earthquakes, unmeltable by lava, uncorrodible by acid.

Most of us have not, of course, experienced anything like the suffering meted out to Etty Hillesum and Viktor Frankl. To even invoke them as admired teachers must be done with care. But I imagine that Etty and Viktor both would want the spirit of their words, forged in the most terrible of circumstances nearly eighty years ago in Czechoslovakia and Poland, to offer solace to someone like me, in Belfast or in North Carolina today. Or to you, wherever you may be. Indeed, isn't it the case that the witness of those who have suffered the most invites those of us who have suffered less to learn from them? Don't we, in some measure, *owe* it to them to live better than we might otherwise? To love others more, to forgive more, to share more? And to love ourselves?

"God won't let you be tested beyond what you can bear" does not mean God won't let them kill you. It means God won't let the deepest reality of who you are be destroyed, even if they *do* kill you. Your part is to choose life even in the face of terror.

EVENTUALLY, THOSE YEARS of despair, misplaced guilt, and unnecessary repentance turned into a gift. Because those torments and confusions were the kinds of insanity that, if it does not destroy your mind, forces you to get out from under it. When religion and culture told me there was something wrong with me because I loved men, they were reversing the truth poles. *They* were claiming to be victims of *my* difference. The oppressor was asking the oppressed to accept responsibility for the oppression and to pretend that the oppression was a gift from God. My mind couldn't take it anymore. So it imploded.

The weight of the conflict between homophobic theology and self-respect was killing me. When the dust settled, I knew I had to drop one of these, and seeing only more (self-)punishment if I stayed, I finally began to extract myself. I defected from the religious structures from which I had received much good but through which I had also internalized the message that I was sick, sinful, even satanic.

None of us deserves the pain this story caused. Unhealthy ideology—the religion of purification, the politics of empire—creates many victims. The first victims, and those who suffer the most, are the scapegoats: the people used by the domination system to build its pyramids, farm its plantations, be its stepping-stones. Such a system denies the body and is so afraid of a god or "the authorities" that it tends to scapegoat and kill rather than accept the complexities of life. Such a system sees people as things, so even the people at the top suffer. Such a system tries to put humans into hierarchies of purity. We must withhold our consent, and whatever privilege we may hold as a result of an unjust system must become the place from which we serve.

Just as the broken parts of systems and the parts that are being redeemed often overlap, in our own personal stories, there isn't usually a clear marker between the damaged places and the healed ones. There was always healing happening, even while the wounding was underway. The great leaps forward were often accompanied by two steps back. Sometimes I would ask myself if I had ever changed at all. And still today I can hear the small, disruptive, biting voice of internalized homophobia. It's quieter now because I've discovered psychologically mature rites of passage and a healthy spiritual community. I have learned that the degree to which we can healthily share our most vulnerable truths is the degree to which our hearers will hold them tenderly, admit the limits of their knowledge, and be accountable for their advice. I also know that talking about our pain unconsciously can retraumatize us but that with wise attention, over time, we can come to a place of rarely needing to talk about it at all. Even more than this, we can learn to share our stories in ways that not only shield us from harm but can help heal others too.

A major facet of my healing began when I took that questionnaire that suggested two yes answers would be indicative of PTSD. When I checked "yes" for thirty-eight of the forty questions, I was finally able to see that not only did I need help but there must be other people like me too. Night terrors, trouble sleeping, constantly replaying frightening experiences in my mind, self-loathing, self-blaming for things other people did: these were never far away.

But now they're not so near to me, and that's because I discovered shelter. You see, shelter is more than four walls and a roof. Shelter, which is the fourth pillar necessary for life, along with food, water, and air, is not just about protection from the physical elements. In these days of screen-mediated engagement with reality, being *overly* sheltered from the elements is actually one of the roots of our sickness. Yet no matter whether we've got the physical part of shelter in place or *too* much in place, we can turn to a deeper form of shelter, the kind that doesn't require walls or a roof at all.

I wrote earlier that a shelter does not defeat the elements but simply makes them irrelevant. And a shelter is a kind of story. It's a blanket we're weaving that covers us, enveloping us in its warmth and hope. A trustable story shelter is a treasure indeed. And a trustable story shelter has three elements: *mentors, calling*, and *community*.

We need *elders and mentors* on the journey: folks who have traveled further on their paths than we have on ours. We need elders who can affirm our gifts, lovingly sandpaper our more unhelpful rough edges, offer a shoulder to cry on and clapping hands to celebrate us, and question us when we're too much in love with our own propaganda.

We need a sense of *calling*: clarity about the place we have in the world, the gift we have received and are invited to share, and work we are here to do for the sake of the common good.

And we need a *community* of people: a group small enough to truly know us, constituted of people committed to the journey of spiritual maturity and service to the common good. In other words, we need a small, merry band of folks dedicated to loving God, neighbor, and self.

LET'S LOOK AT each of these three aspects of a sturdy story shelter.

Mentors. Mentors are often older than we are. But sometimes they are peers: intimate friends with whom we can share the most painful troughs and smile the smile of recognition—that while a part of all pain must be undergone alone, there is no pain that has not also been experienced by another. Sometimes they are the people with whom we most deeply share our lives and are still safe. Whoever they are and however long they remain present, the truest mentors are the ones who love you without personal gain, who invest in you with healthy boundaries, and who know that while they may not be around to see the harvest of what they have sown, what they are transferring to you will benefit generations hence.

Sometimes they are medicine people—like Dave the Therapist, with whom I spent three years learning to breathe, and to walk, and to talk in ways that would expand

and not contract me. I learned to hold the past tenderly so that my painful memories would no longer be a grenade whose pin had disappeared, leaving me shaking as I tried to hold it closed.

Dave taught me that sometimes talking about our pain is the worst thing we can do with it. Until we have learned to tap into the part of ourselves that is bigger than the pain and to be gentle with how our bodies have retained trauma, merely talking about it might simply repeat it. The tracks have been laid down by the monsters in our heads, and we will keep traveling those same tracks until we put someone else in charge of the signal box. But the miracle of how the human brain works is that we can, with assistance both loving and wise, step off the tracks that have been restricting us to the path of self-rejection. We can lay new tracks, even as the train moves. The first step is to slow down the train enough to pick up some new wood.

Some days are better than others, and so we travel slowly, building the track as we go with wood we retrieve from the forest that borders the path. Sometimes that wood will come from mentors who show us areas of the forest we haven't entered before. That was certainly the case with the trauma therapy I experienced. Sometimes we will pause to look around, seeing the place where the sensitivity induced by our wounds meets the needs of the world. We will often find important information there about who we really are and what we are here for.

Community. I have learned that I cannot do this alone. I have learned to gather in circles of between three to twelve people and to dive deep into the questions of what matters.*

We ask each other what is bringing us life, and we learn to do more of that. We ask each other what is not bringing

---

* See the idea for creating a Porch Circle at the end of chapter 11.

us life, and we learn to do less of that. We ask each other how we are experiencing our sense of calling to the common good, and we encourage and challenge each other for the impacts of our lives.

We ask each other how we can help. And then we help.

Calling. The third element of a story shelter is to discern a sense of purpose within yourself that will serve the common good. In my experience, there is only one way to find your purpose. You must go into the deepest source of your pain and come through the other side. Only then can you look back and see the mythic dimensions of what happened to you and how you might be a vessel for healing the same thing in others. This, truly, is what it means to *seize the day* or *be all you can be*: not selfish ambition or conquest but service to the world, and enjoyment of it, from your truest self.

OF COURSE I have been, and am, selfish. Of course I participate in separation stories, not fully welcoming, not fully loving. Of course I am acquainted with legitimate sources of regret for my mistakes. A kind of holy shame can be necessary to turn the conscience toward taking responsibility for the impact of my own self-regard. Defining the difference between holy and toxic shame is actually quite simple. When it's honest and proportionate, "I've done something bad" can be a holy beginning of taking responsibility and making amends. But "I am bad" is toxic. We're probably all experiencing some mix of both holiness and toxicity much of the time.

Yet our wounds, when they are being healed, and our gifts, when they are coming into bloom, will dance with each other. This dance is always available, and participating in it is actually the way to most fully experience life. Sometimes spiritual growth is excruciating, like new teeth pushing through gums far too fast, and sometimes it's exhilarating, like the first time taking off in a plane. It's a dance. You can decline if you want, but this room in which we live is going to be full of music regardless. Why not join the dance?

Repress the wound and it will fester, preventing your own healing and often seeping into the lives of those around you. Jump into the gifts without humility and you might find yourself becoming a kind of stage magician who can saw a person in half but never experience the delicious liberation of knowing that it's not about you. Having gifts without developing the maturity to use them might leave you with a half-sawed person you can't put back together again.

But if you can dip your toes into a more whole way of being, you might discover the formula for a healthy mix of wound and gift. Your wound might begin to transform—first into a scar and then into a superpower. Indeed, you might find that you always had what you needed but were just never initiated into knowing it.

EVENTUALLY, JUST AS most of us have experienced trauma as an unwelcome initiation, we must be *initiated* onto the path of integration. Calling on myths and archetypes can radically deepen the reintegration of our wounded memories and help heal the fear that we'll be broken forever. It's no wonder that original wounds often seem mythic. In trauma, ancient energies of human misdeeds and animal nature are being reenacted; in fact, one reason traumatic memory often seems "monstrous" is that, in mythic terms, monsters were actually there.

I was surrounded by a group of older boys, tied to a tree, and threatened with a knife. It's not exactly Prometheus strapped to a rock with an eagle sent to eat his liver, a liver that grows back overnight, only for the eagle to return the next day and eat some more. But the myth helps. It helps me honor the real pain I experienced: the terror, the misplaced shame, the sense that the memory never had long enough to heal before another set of talons would come along and tear the wound open again. It also speaks to my desire to be sensitive toward those who may feel that *I* arrived in *their* life as an eagle—those who, because I had not integrated the damaged little boy, I wounded.

Remember that this is not a story about "good guys" and "bad guys." We have each been on both sides of wounding. And we can all heal. But no matter how small your story may seem to you in the scheme of things, if the wound seemed mythic, the healing must be mythic too. This may be one of the least understood aspects of how to find authentic ease in life, but it's been hiding in plain sight, in the work of one of the most authentic people who ever lived. The teachings of Swiss psychiatrist and psychoanalyst Carl Jung, like those of so many prophetic wisdom figures from around the world, have been diluted through being institutionalized and packaged for quicker consumption. But beneath the surface, there is the truth of possibly incomparable power.

Jung showed that our commonplace distress can often only be healed by moving our frame of reference—you could think of it as the dimensions of our story shelter—*up and out, down and in.* We must move toward the perception of how our little lives are woven with each other and with the cosmos. He called these "supra-personal connections." In other words, and at the risk of oversimplifying, sometimes to solve a problem, we need to make it bigger. There are dragons, and in each life, some dragon slaying will be necessary. We must take care not to identify the people who may have hurt us (or ourselves) with the monsters. Befriending the mythic dimension within can enable us to slay dragons without harming any other humans.

There are several ways we could talk about this transformation, and the most helpful I have found is in the idea that each person contains a sea brimming with archetypes. Familiar in ancient myths and most famously explored by Jung, archetypes can manifest in shadow or light. We can call them energies, or emphases, or lenses through which we see the world. We must be careful not to overidentify with archetypes. Instead, I prefer to see them as doorways through which we can walk on the path toward claiming our truest selves. Over time, we can learn how to place each doorway in front of the other so that we're walking through all of them at once.

When it comes to naming archetypes, theories differ. Some use four archetypes, some nine or twelve, some refer to archetypal *events* such as birth, marriage, and death, and wisdom can be found in all those ways of seeing. The most helpful archetypal lens for me is fourfold: we are all lovers, sovereigns, warrior-protectors, and magicians. We all *feel*, like a lover does; we all *choose*, as a ruler does; we all have *boundaries*, which a warrior-protector holds; and we all *transform* the world, as a magician can. We are all called to love, to decide, to protect, to transform. The question is whether or not we will bring consciousness and accountability to the embodiment of these archetypes. Will we remember what is truly within us, and will we choose to be answerable for how we live into this immense power? If consciousness and accountability remain unawakened, instead of living a life of courage, creativity, and beauty toward the common good, we risk the greatest tragedy: a life dominated by unconscious shadow that contributes to separation, scapegoating, and selfishness. Here's what this can mean.

When stepping into the energy of the lover, will we allow ourselves to cleanly feel the range of emotions, from intense grief to delirious joy? Or will we seduce others, manifesting as a bottomless pit of need?

When sovereign power is called for, will we choose and lead for the common good, or will we be tyrants?

When warrior-protector energy is necessary, will we shield the vulnerable and exhaust nonviolent options while being willing to suffer ourselves? Or will we enact dominance, unnecessary force, and violence?

When the alchemy of a magician is invited, will we turn lead into gold, creating change that benefits the common good? Or will we manipulate the world to get only what we selfishly want?

In short, inside us all is a source of immense power—to love, to decide, to protect, to transform—that can be used for the common good or for personal gain. These four archetypal energies can be channeled with glorious light or demonic shadow. Will we use them to help heal the realm in which we move or sicken it?

As we think about the wound and the gift, we can ask ourselves how to offer healing to others of the very kind we did not receive ourselves. And as we lay the wood, we may discover that the track can go to places we never thought possible.

Seeking mentors, listening for the calling, and sharing in community are useful steps that will often lead us to the edge of the initiation we need. Such initiation may be painful in parts, yet this time, we will welcome it.

I USED TO believe I was permanently broken and toxic to those around me. To myself. I once found it difficult to carry little else but the pain of that belief.

It took me to the end of myself. I went into the deep, dark forest of self-abandonment. I discovered what it is like to hate myself (or at least the *story* that I believed was myself). As long as I isolated, I could pretend that the pain was mine alone. Of course, there were always people who loved me and wanted the best for me. My isolation from them caused them sorrow, and it prevented me from discovering my power, gifts, and purpose. Because only in conscious relationship with others could I see my impact, for good and ill. Wounded relationships taught me that I could, in the end, hurt people. That my actions mattered. That I could love and work magic. But without a mature sovereign ready to make decisions that might cost me and without an inner warrior-protector ready to hold boundaries rather than let them be trampled, love and magic would easily corrode into codependency and self-deception.

Good medicine came in the form of good mentors, who would affirm and challenge me, and in the form of good trauma therapy.

Accountability came in the form of a community who cheered me on and with whom I share needs and gifts. These things helped me uncover the unshakeable core beneath the core that I thought was broken.

Now I can remember the tree, and I can smile, for that little boy no longer needs to remain tied up, threatened, and alone.

He is loved. He has an entirely whole, older brother in the me that I am today. The adult me is holding his hand, telling him he is loved and beautiful and perfectly good.

He is not a pawn. He has a king watching from within and over him, seeing the damage about to be done, and saying, *Stop. This is wrong. I'm going to take care of you. Here's what we're going to do.*

He will be defended. He has a warrior-protector walking alongside him, ready to step in between his vulnerability and the bullies. Ready to use power to force the bullies back.

His pain will be transformed. And he has a magician who transforms the moment, and the entire world, by offering healing not only to him but to the bully also.

When integrated, these four archetypes become a whole person. One who feels it all and is not submerged. One who stands up for what is right and is not a killer. One who sees what needs to be done and makes it happen. One who turns lead into gold and shares it.

You see, the old adage that we should be the change we wish to see in the world does not only refer to what we call politics—although it most certainly does that. It's about something even closer than whether we vote or march or run for office, even closer than how we treat the neighbors who live on our very streets. It's about how we treat ourselves. Be the change you wish to see in *yourself.*

While we look for external mentors, we are also invited to learn how to mentor *ourselves* from our own inner wisdom. And we must. And while we can certainly look for community, we are also invited to befriend *ourselves.* And we must.

Life is difficult. Though not always. Obsessively rushing to "win" at all costs is a *really* difficult way to live. And always.

To be a member of what we now call the LGBTQ+ community means to be a recipient of gifts and an heir to suffering. There have been generations of murder, literal and figurative, as the wider culture has projected its own angst about bodies, about intimacy, about vulnerability, and about what it means to be a man or a woman onto the bodies and spirits of beautiful people who were merely trying to love. Generations of murder. We feel it in our bones.

And there have been generations of gift—without the wisdom and art of my queer ancestors, our aesthetic and familial reservoirs might be nearly empty.

You do not need to be a member of the LGBTQ+ community or any other marginalized community for your pain to be valid or your gifts welcome. Many of us hold overlapping memberships in various communities; many of us are privileged and marginalized at the same time, depending on which part of us we are looking at. No doubt some folks suffer more than others, but competing in the pain Olympics gets us nowhere. What matters is living with integrity from the power we hold and serving the places where other people do not. We are evolving to a place where the gifts of historically persecuted and marginalized people are finally being centered. There are wounds to heal and amends to be made by those responsible. The responsibility of being human includes asking yourself what power you have, how you can use it for the common good, and how you can make amends for ways you may have misused it. What lack do you have, and who are the safe people you can ask for help?

So give yourself the gift of self-declaration. Fearlessly own your privilege, and tenderly face your lack. Open yourself to archetypal initiation. There is a gift here that can enable you not only to live better than you ever thought possible but also, when the time comes, to die as if it were living too.

The Fifth Way to Not Be Afraid: Imagine What Your Wiser Self Would Tell You

A WISE MAN once led me in an exercise that he called Crossroads. I don't know where he learned the exercise, and if I find out, I'll tell you. You might want to try it yourself.

Select three objects—any household item will suffice. Place two chairs by walls at least twenty paces apart, facing each other. Sit in one of the chairs. Eyes closed, breathing slowly, call to mind the faces of the people you admire the most; it's not important whether you've met them or whether they're real or fictional. Imagine them sitting in the chair opposite you. Let their faces blend into each other, as if a series of translucent masks are placed on top of each other.

Then allow an image of your face to blend into theirs until what remains is the face of an elder, made up of the wisdom you find in the stories you've learned. The summation of elder wisdom, looking at you through your eyes.

Imagine yourself to be this wise elder at the end of a long life, with the archetypes in balance, no longer striving to compete or achieve, aware of flaws and gifts both, and seeing their younger self—you—with the eyes of grace.

Ask yourself the following, and speak out loud, and write down the characteristics of this wise elder: this wiser you. What are they like? What age are they? What are their priorities? What do they *know*?

Ask yourself what this wise elder—this wise you—might want to say to you at earlier moments in your life: when you were a young child, a teenager, a young adult, before you hit forty, or whatever stages in life you need healing.

Ask yourself what this wise elder might want to say to you now, at this moment in your life. Ask yourself what they might tell you about yourself. Ask yourself what they might teach you. Might they warn you of anything? Encourage you? Reassure you?

Ask this wise elder, this wise you, What are the three obstacles between who you are now and who they have become? Pause.

Place the three objects on the floor between your chair and the one in which you are imagining the wise elder is sitting. Imagine that each one represents one of the three obstacles between who you are now and the wiser, older version of yourself.

Move toward the wise elder slowly, and pay attention to the obstacles. Perhaps pick them up. Become aware of their shape, weight, and size. Place them down again, and move past them.

And when you arrive at the opposite chair, slowly and with sacred attention, take your seat, imagining the wise elder welcoming you into the inheritance you have helped shape for yourself.

Sit there quietly for a few minutes. And when you're ready, inquire of the wise elder, the wise you. To become like this wise elder, what are three things you need to do today, and next week, and this year?

Speak these things aloud, and write them down, and do them.

chapter 11

fear of the world

The main thing that privileged
people have lost in the past few
years is a false sense of certainty
about the future.

—Mahan Siler

FOR YEARS AFTER the signing of a negotiated treaty between
the factions in northern Ireland, guns were on everyone's mind.
In those days, after the Good Friday / Belfast Agreement in
1998, it seemed that there was no higher principle than what you
thought about guns. We talked endlessly about where the guns
were, who had them, and why they weren't being given up.

In the summer of 2000, two prime ministers hoped we would
talk some more. Men and women who may have thought that
they represented ancient warrior traditions were moving toward
an end to the war, if not the fight. The prime ministers came,
they spent a week, and they may have thought they had conquered. I was living right beside Stormont Castle's government
buildings at the time—a stone's throw from where my future
was being decided. I would drive out of my house and find that

my view of the castle buildings was obscured by satellite dishes, evidence that the world's media also considered us worthy of a week's attention.

I had felt enthusiastic about but somewhat disempowered by the peace process, excluded from deciding what kind of society I was going to live in. I had helped found a little organization dedicated to being part of changing the story about northern Ireland. We invited political leaders to speak in churches from the "other" community, sought to take personal responsibility for challenging bigotry, and supported people making meaningful connections across borders that had been established in mutual suspicion. Some people even moved into neighborhoods where their very difference might help dilute the myth of "us" and "them." It was a heady time of exciting activism. We were making up the strategy as we went along, but the principle was clear: if the rules of a society, written or unwritten, induce people to hurt each other, you should make better rules.

By the time I was twenty-five years old, I was really tired of the rules. The cease-fires had led to political negotiations, and an ensuing referendum endorsed the establishment of a power-sharing government, the release of paramilitary prisoners, the decommissioning of illegally held weapons, the reform of the police, and some of the most advanced human rights and equality legislation in the world. But we still couldn't find a way to make it all work. Each side of the conflict interpreted the agreement in ways that emphasized their own success. Each seemed unwilling to make the compromises necessary to allow their opponents to seal the deal.

By the summer of 2000, no government was in sight. In collective frustration, a group of variously well-adjusted peace activists traveled to Stormont, getting to the gates late one evening. We didn't really know why we were there other than the fact that we knew we wanted—needed—to have some impact on what was being decided about our lives. Inside the gates, the politicians, including the two prime ministers, were talking about peace. The security guard told us that he wasn't supposed to let anyone in at that time of night; we told him that all we wanted to do was pray.

Sometimes I think it works. I can't comprehensively define prayer, but it does seem more necessary to do it than to understand it. It's not merely—or even mostly—about asking for things. Instead, I think prayer is joining what's already unfolding in the spirit of authority and love, protecting vulnerable people and the earth, and being willing to *act* with that spirit.

Back at the Stormont gates, the guard said that he thought that praying was probably a better idea than whatever the politicians up the hill were suggesting and that he would let us in as long as we didn't tell anyone. That sounded good to us, so we walked about a mile to Castle Buildings, where we thought we might take our action. When we got there, police officers told us they weren't allowed to let anyone inside the perimeter fence unless they were either participants in the talks or members of the press. So we stood outside and prayed in a circle—a slightly-embarrassed-but-not-knowing-what-else-to-do circle—wondering if all we were going to get that night was a better view of the satellite dishes.

Shortly thereafter, our prayers were answered when an anti-peace process politician saw us and came out to ask what we were doing there. We told him that we were praying for peace and that the police wouldn't let us in. He responded that the presence of politicians from across the spectrum, conflict combatants, and the media from so many different countries made it seem remiss "that citizens like yourself could be excluded."

I spoke up, wanting to make sure that he knew we weren't there to support his party's position. He said he understood that but that it was our constitutional right to meet our assembly members, so he would bring us in. It's arguable, of course, whether or not our presence that evening was helpful, but I have always appreciated the fact that a political opponent was willing to respect human decency before party position. We went in, we prayed, we talked to politicians who disagreed with us, we moved on. The next day, we went back and met the two prime ministers. As one does.

The Irish taoiseach Bertie Ahern and the British prime minister Tony Blair came out to meet us, our community now mingling with a group of mothers with small children, each of us there to encourage the historic connection across lines of enmity that we knew to be possible but was still uncertain. Blair was formal, not as relaxed as he seemed on TV; Ahern was as comfy as a used car salesman. They must have both been exhausted, and while the photo opportunity with some ordinary folks calling for extraordinary change (and willing to change ourselves as well) was too good to miss, I imagine they might have wanted to be elsewhere. The Blair handshake was stiff too; the Ahern grip felt like the preliminary stage of a bear hug between old friends. I took Bertie aside and asked him what was going on in the building behind us. He said, "Ah, it's just this aul decommissioning thing; if we get that sorted, then we'll be all right."

Tony continued to shake hands—the women with children in strollers, a few of us youngish people, waiting for a word. "Ahem. Thank you for coming," he said and then cleared his throat again. "Thank you for coming." He patted the head of a little girl nearby. She looked up at him and said, in the kind of squeaky voice you associate with Disney films, "Mr. Blair, I have a question. Are you going to make peace, or are you not going to make peace?"

The prime minister looked past the little girl to the adults, his palm still on her head, and reminded us of how even the most powerful people are often just as bewildered as the rest of us, not to mention under a great deal more pressure, pronouncing after another throat clearing, "Well, that *is* the question."

FOR SOME OF us, that question is always there. Are you going to make peace or not? It's not just a question for prime ministers. It should be directed inwardly too. Not merely to admonish us but because it points the way to overcoming our fear of the world—that the terror that what's going on *out there* is unstoppable. Whether it takes five minutes or five decades, we think that eventually the monsters will come for us. Sometimes the monsters are enormous: the one closest to me is an eight-hundred-year-long conflict over how the island I'm from should be governed and how its people should treat each other. For the place now known as the United States, the monster could be defined as the legacy of what was done to the original inhabitants and the people brought there in chains as well as the beliefs that were (and sometimes still are) used to legitimize those actions. Beyond that, people all over the world may face the monsters of war, pandemics, violence on the streets or in the schools, authoritarian power, societal collapse, ecological devastation, the threatened end of the human race. Sometimes the monsters are smaller: family tension, loss of income or reputation, illness, being publicly shamed or run over by a bus. The size of the monster doesn't matter, for even a mosquito can kill. What matters is that, for some of us, it is always there: the fear that the world is just too full of trouble and that we cannot do anything about it. That external forces are just too much.

This *thing* that might happen to us feels, for some, closer than our own skin. Indeed, it literally changes our very bodies— pelts feel tight, pulse rates rise, headaches overcome, eyes fog. The experience of fear is, of course, not always this intense, but it is universal. We all know fear. We fear suffering, both the physical and emotional kinds. We fear loss, of loved ones and dreams. We fear being alone. We fear not having enough. We fear having meaningless lives. We sometimes fear the world and our place in it. We fear death. Fear threatens to have the whole thing pretty well sewn up, from emergence to fade out. If we don't learn how to work with it, fear can rule our lives.

Some of us are plagued by fear of such an intensity that we have built walls around ourselves: fortresses of the mind and heart designed to protect but that in reality keep us from experiencing love. Some of us are so wounded by events that we have retreated into a self-perpetuating cycle of anxiety. We fear the world, so we avoid the world and never see how lovely and unfrightening the world can be. Some of us have been so punished by the fear-inducing voices in our heads that we have convinced ourselves that we would not even know where to *begin* to heal.

And this is the second gift of fear, because eventually the waste of life that accompanies fear will provoke enough desperation that we demand change. We all eventually ask for help, whether in the moment of immediate crisis or at the end of a broken life. We know that it would be better if we did it now, but in some less enlightened parts of our culture, there is a powerful urge to resist asking for help. Asking for help is too often taken to be a sign of weakness, despite evidence to the contrary.

Until a global pandemic came along, that is, and revealed as never before our interdependency not just in our neighborhoods but across the planet. Our global crises—not only the pandemic—are in large part the consequence of leaders adopting and perpetuating the culture of separation and pretend invulnerability, claiming egotistical and nationalistic dominance, unwilling to admit our interdependency as a species—and an ecosystem—lest it seem that our own sectarian group or nation or religion is not the be-all and end-all that our pride cracks it up to be. It is also the consequence of people believing those lies and of the alternatives not being presented creatively enough to seem credible. We have seen the consequences, today and throughout history: people or nations that "go it alone" often end up very dangerous—and very lonely—indeed.

And the converse is true. Deciding to walk the path with companions doesn't just make the journey less lonely and more agreeable; the intimacy of traveling with others is part of what makes life livable. Indeed, every successful movement for good reveals that the secret of happiness lies in two mutually reinforcing actions: We find our true selves through stillness, and we deepen our interdependence with others. And repeat. The experience of asking for (and being asked for) help doesn't just help the person asking but heals the helper too. In that regard, a person asking for help should be celebrated. Asking for help is the first step toward disentangling yourself from the oppression of your own fear, the first step toward unlocking your potential to love yourself, and finally the first step toward liberating your gift to the human race. When you truly ask for help, you're no longer a danger to yourself, or to me, or to the world.

THE PSYCHOLOGIST STEVEN Pinker says that "there are two ways to understand the world: a constant drip of anecdotes about the worst things that have happened anywhere on the planet in the previous hour, or a bird's-eye view of the grand developments that are transforming the human condition. The first is called 'the news,' and for your wisdom and mental health I recommend balancing it with the second." Pinker would be the first to note that this is only part of the story. Reality is more complex than his statement might imply, because some of the developments in the world may be transforming the human condition for the worse, and there are some places in particular where change cannot come a moment too soon. However, let's not miss the core truth intended here: headlines and trendlines are not the same thing. I wonder if those of us who are afraid of the world just don't know it well enough. The world, that is. Indeed, we may *think* we know it *too much*, and too much exposure to the world's shadows may have overwhelmed us, but we can easily lose sight of the whole.

We may react against this notion because we see so much horror around us, on TV screens and the internet, in the air. But these are often manifestations of the availability bias wherein we predict probability based on how easily we can recall similar examples. We see lots of violence in the media so we predict that violence is ever increasing and coming ever closer. But the mainstream news media has not yet weaned itself off the disaster capitalism principle that violence sells and the ensuing dogma that conflict is more newsworthy than its absence. Much mainstream storytelling—in the "news," movies and television, literature, music, and games—has not typically reported the *absence* of violence or other unhealthy conflict as even more compelling than their presence. There are some hopeful signs that that is changing, along with the expansion of the range of voices who are invited to speak within mainstream storytelling contexts. The learning curve will be more complete when the default in public storytelling about violence and conflict and other sources that stimulate fear is to illustrate the context in which they occur, the long-term effects, and the widespread and often successful attempts at their transformation. We might promote the goal that in the future, the average person would be historically and statistically literate about conflicts that have been transformed into peace processes. We don't have to limit this goal to how we talk about *group* conflict—it can only help to share stories about how less violence has been used to prevent or repair more, whether between or within nations, across lines of religious or ethnic or political belonging, within families or between people who just bumped into each other on the street.

The problem is not that creative nonviolence and imaginative storytelling for the common good have been tried and failed but that when they are tried, *we don't talk about it enough!* One day, stories of overcoming separation, scapegoating, selfishness, and violence through creative common good activism and better storytelling might be told in such a spellbinding way that each of us will know as many stories of creative transformation as we previously heard stories of destruction. We might each learn steps we could take to help transform our communities, nations, and the planet for the better. And perhaps one day, too, we will no longer endorse an economic model that enriches institutions and individuals dedicated to selling advertising through fearful spectacle and exploiting human suffering; we could begin by withholding our financial support for such institutions right now.

At any rate, it's still quicker to report looting by a few than to truly listen to mass peaceful protest, tell the stories of the deep work of restorative justice, or highlight the organizations dedicated to the common good. So the active terrors that do exist find their way into our unchecked consciousness more easily than the growth of a new forest, reductions in violence, the expansion of human rights, and the evolution of love. Ironically, the fact that we pay attention to the violence that is reported might itself be a manifestation of love—that is, part of why we pay attention may be because empathy is becoming more affirmed as a way of looking at the world. In the expanding circle of empathy, we have been given a gift, but we haven't learned how to use it yet. We often falsely perceive and overstate the limited violence in our world as if it were constantly increasing, but part of the reason we do so is because many of us now care more about a wider range of other human beings than we used to. There are at least two unfortunate consequences to the false premise that things are always getting worse. First is that our fear multiplies our perception of threat, which itself nurtures the foundations for more violence. Second is that our misperceptions more easily lend themselves to disempowerment rather than galvanizing the kind of movement that transforms the world for the better. In other words, if the problems are insurmountable, why try to surmount them? We are stunned into inaction, and the circle goes around and around. But when we look at the reasons why violence reduces, we may be greeted by not only hope but empowerment.

Violence reduces when women are empowered. If you are a person, you can participate in the empowerment of women today: learn about gender injustice and how you benefit or suffer from it, promote women's voices, and if you're a cisgender man, assume that you have unearned advantages that can only be redeemed by being shared.

Violence reduces when states evolve democracy. If you are a person, you can participate in shaping democracy today: register to vote, run for office, do what you can to achieve ranked voting systems that more accurately represent the people, work to transform policing and military institutions toward accountable public safety and peacemaking services.

Violence reduces when public discourse promotes mutual respect between people and values public figures for service to the common good rather than their dominance. This has something to do with treating each other as others would like to be treated. If you are a person, you can reduce violence today by treating just one other person as you would like to be treated and by withholding your consent—and money—from systems that scapegoat or humiliate others.

Violence reduces when storytelling matures. The emergence of the novel coincided with significant reductions in violence, because of its power as a mass storytelling method to inspire empathy, inviting readers to see the world from the perspective of another. If you are a person, you can learn to tell stories in ways that increase empathy—both within yourself and in the hearts and minds of those listening.

In the future, people may speak of our moment in history as being characterized not by war and endless conflict but by repeated manifestations of a revolution for the better in how human beings treat each other and the earth. The core beneath the core in every human being is an essential connection with all living things; when one part suffers, all suffer. When one part heals, all heal. There is far more to the world than fighting to win. The arc of the moral universe may well bend toward justice, but as Barbara Holmes says, "It depends on our participation. What is your work today to bend the universe a little more towards justice?" Whether or not you're reading this in a future moment of greater political ease, social healing, and beloved community, your task while here will be the same. Your task, your privilege, your gift is to overcome your fear of the world by becoming the very thing your true self knows the world needs.

NONE OF THIS is to diminish the real impact of violence. Far from it. We mourn with those who mourn. But violence does not reduce when we exaggerate it. On the contrary, as we've already noted, exaggerating the amount of violence leads to either increased perception of threat (which produces more violence) or excess powerlessness (which does nothing to reduce violence).

One of the first things many northern Irish people of my generation remember is a parent looking under the car to see if there was a bomb there. The next thing is more stories of death, and more, and more, and more. You would think, looking back, that killing was the only thing that happened in the northern Ireland of my childhood. But it wasn't. We were living through the tail end of a civil conflict that was eight hundred years in the making. Every killing was a universe, of course, and a nightmare. But every act of peacemaking made a new story possible.

It was the end of something, not the beginning. The wounds of neighbor pitted against neighbor are real, and none of the killing was worth it. Seen up close and personal, it could feel like all we had was conflict. But from a distance, I grew up in beauty. The Giant's Causeway. Seapark. Donaghadee. The Mournes. Ballycastle. Open fireplaces. Glenlyon. The accents. The languages. The music. The support for the grieving, the sharing of burdens, the yearning for a better way. The people. And the attempts made over decades to resolve the conflict nonviolently finally paid off. Former sworn enemies now share power. Moves continue to help people make peace with the past. We promise to never do such things again. And as we seek to integrate the wounds and the fear with the community and the healing, we understand that the key is to try to tell the story in a way that produces more light than heat. The same is true wherever you are. Stories that increase a sense of threat often end up producing more harm. Most of them also happen to be inaccurate. Stories that decrease a sense of threat often end up reducing harm. Most of them also happen to be true.

IS IT NOT possible to respond justly to terror without reenacting it? How do we address the real issues of injustice that, ostensibly or literally, lay behind the northern Ireland conflict, the September 11 attacks, authoritarian aggression, and every other act of violent lashing out against others? How can we do this without providing cover for terrorism or abusive political regimes? How do we see beyond the caricatures of evil and into people's hearts and minds? Should we even try? How do we challenge the military-industrial-entertainment complex, so bent on militarism and quick, cathartic, and often destructive "fixes" rather than the things that make for peace? How can those of us with power in our society step out from behind the privilege that protects us to act in solidarity with those who are vulnerable? What can we do to nurture an imagination that will teach us how to transform conflict without making it worse?

The answer is to tell a new story. And the new story will emerge from the old one.

The key here is to seek the most *truthful* version of the story, which means examining headlines in their contexts: of history, culture, and who is doing the telling. One example may be that the trend is toward reduced violence and increased peace, but this has occurred only because human beings have challenged codes and practices that were considered unchangeable. The mass barbarism of execution for public entertainment, the elitist madness of "resolving" wounded honor by duels, the horrific subjugation and even killing of people with physical differences because they were believed by many to be worthless: all these things once seemed normal. The most ordinary people responded to their circumstances by deciding to act: to stop what once had seemed immovable but now could no longer be tolerated. We will do the same, but not by waiting on social forces to do the work for us. For today's social pressures, conflicts, and opportunities are invitations to transformative action, not unchangeable blueprints for the future.

As Rabbi Michael Lerner says, Martin Luther King Jr. is not known for a speech entitled "I Have a Complaint"—although he did squarely critique the injustices of his time, most strikingly what he called the evil triplets of racism, militarism, and materialism. Beyond unambiguous critique, however, he outlined a vision to overcome them. Because that vision is so rarely articulated beyond platitudes and often reduced to the famous statement that people "would not be judged by the color of their skin but on the content of their character," it's important to elaborate. The vision of Beloved Community, coined by Josiah Royce (founder of the Fellowship of Reconciliation) and enlarged by Dr. King, "is a global vision, in which all people can share in the wealth of the earth. In the Beloved Community, poverty, hunger and homelessness will not be tolerated because international standards of human decency will not allow it. Racism and all forms of discrimination, bigotry and prejudice will be replaced by an all-inclusive spirit of sisterhood and brotherhood. In the Beloved Community, international disputes will be resolved by peaceful conflict-resolution and reconciliation of adversaries, instead of military power. Love and trust will triumph over fear and hatred. Peace with justice will prevail over war and military conflict." Dr. King was no longer willing to tolerate the injustices of his time and did not allow the scale of the task or the risk to his life prevent him following the path of his true self, aiming for and cocreating Beloved Community, one step after another. The movement he led responded to the fear of the world not with oppositional energy but by rising to overcome the old order with a vision of something new and better.

It was ever thus. Every generation has the opportunity to become sensitized to the injustice whose time has come. For ours, it might be white supremacy, the dehumanization of people on account of who they love, capital punishment, human trafficking, or the encroachment of the national security state. It might be the evils of earth exploitation, the systematic exclusion of people on grounds of the money they don't have, or the trading practices that deliver cheap products to some of us while keeping the hands that make them tied to a wheel of exhaustion or worse.

For me, it is the way our culture tells the story that violence resolves conflict by redeeming it. Our real religion is the god of violence, the demonic notion that killing can create things. Yet violence is never constructive, even in the extremely limited circumstances where it may be arguably necessary.

Violence doesn't create anything.

That's a radioactive statement. When I say it in certain circles, the reaction is swift and unambiguous. It's ironic that conversation about reducing violence often results in a fight, but even that fight proves the point: violence doesn't *create* anything. Except suffering, of course.

People react to this suggestion with such intense opposition for a number of reasons. We have been told from the earliest age the opposite: that violence works and that violent sacrifice is noble. We have been taught, through our national and community rituals, not only that our "freedoms" were secured by the deaths of our forebears (and the killing they carried out) but that such death and killing was the only way it could have happened. We have been nurtured into a catechism of fearing the

world so that we must always have violence as a recourse because we never know when they are going to target *us*. If such
premises were true, it's perfectly reasonable to live fearful and
ready to kill.

But the premises are false.

The suffering caused by violence, even in the noblest of causes,
does not end when the shooting stops. World War I left a divided
Balkan people, laying the foundations for their grandchildren
and great-grandchildren to perpetrate or suffer genocide seventy
years later. The vengeance-fueled response to Germany after that
war laid the foundations for the rise of Nazism. The "resolution" of
World War II allowed Stalin to kill more people than Hitler. The
refusal of political opponents to talk to each other in northern Ireland perpetuated the terms of our conflict for decades, eventually
killing nearly four thousand and physically injuring at least forty-
seven thousand people. And when the talking started, the killing
radically reduced and has been reducing ever since we started to
imagine our destinies as more interdependent than exclusive and
choose to act accordingly.

The sacrifices that gained our "freedom"—whatever "freedom" is supposed be—were indeed costly. Some of them were
certainly noble, especially when they involved people giving
their lives to protect the vulnerable or when they were carried
out by people who had no choice in the matter. But the idea that
only violence makes the nation free is disproven in the historical
fact that nonviolent revolutions produce more democracy than
violent attempts at political change. The cost of talking to the
person who killed your loved one, the cost of forgoing revenge
in exchange for the common good, the cost of not getting everything you want: these are, of course, not easy. But they often
work, and they work far more often than violence, aggressive
expansion, and scapegoating do.

The threat of the world today is lied about every time you
open your computer or switch on your phone. Terror lives in your

pocket, on a device that does not differentiate between wisdom, information, propaganda, and deceit. The good news is that you can also learn more than ever before, connect more quickly, and heal yourself. (Some of the world's great healers and healing techniques are found on mobile apps.) The challenge—and the invitation—is that you need to learn how to edit what you're seeing. No one else will do that for you. Indeed, it is in the interests of the military-industrial-entertainment-gossip complex that you stay unconscious and click on as many links as possible.

The current global crisis is a crisis of storytelling. We have become possessed by the myth of redemptive violence: the belief that violence creates order out of chaos. When we tell the story that way, fear becomes exaggerated and violence increases. The *redemption* of the myth of redemptive violence is not to destroy it by beating the "bad guys" at their own game. No, the redemption of the myth of redemptive violence is to "de-story" it: to refuse to play the game at all. To invent a new game. If we tell the story in a way that decreases fear, violence will reduce.

IT'S NOT A sin to feel afraid of the world. In fact, it's quite natural, given both our evolutionary past as the targets of saber-toothed tigers and the contemporary immersive information culture that implies such beasts are still waiting around every corner. Many of us also have stories of real suffering from our own personal narratives, and the way we have learned to remember and talk about these stories keeps us reliving the trauma, endlessly looking for a way out but never finding it.

Our cultural conditioning confuses us about how to survive and integrate and move beyond trauma. Culture contains some of the seeds of our healing: there is more elevating art and literature and medicine and nature and human kindness than can be experienced in even a thousand lifetimes. However, the current economic model that drives information and creative media is addicted to overemphasizing horror, separation, selfishness, and scapegoating.

I used to be terrified of everything because I bought the lie that we lived in hell and that the monsters who ruled there were unconquerably bigger than me. Even many of the brave peacemakers were burdened by the story that our world was a sinking ship and that our only recourse was to bucket out as much water as we could. What we didn't realize was that the ship had already sunk. The patterns of relationship upon which our divided land was built could never serve us. The very existence of the place legally called "Northern Ireland" was built on scarcity and fear, overdosed on mutual enmity (or at least mutual ignorance), and enshrined hierarchies intended to keep one community happy and the other compliant, which turned out to be self-sabotaging. By promoting a winner-takes-all politics, making one community in charge while refusing the other any meaningful stake, we helped create a textbook example of how not to live with difference. And in the end, by delaying the path of interdependent community through the madness of defining our interests as keeping people out rather than welcoming each other, we delayed our own healing. One majority group dominating a minority large enough to organize in opposition is a recipe only for conflict. So the reason the ship had already sunk is that it was never a seaworthy vessel in the first place. We needed another boat. Today, and likely for some time to come, peacemakers from across the political spectrum are engaged in the task of building it. A boat on which a better story can be told. Of course, northern Ireland will have its own particular subplots and characters and imaginative discourses, as will any other place. But for most of us, wherever we're from, the better story will acknowledge that while we may see fifteen thousand fictionalized murders by the age of sixteen, if we learn to be conscious about *how* we look, we will see a lot more flowers bloom than that. And if we get really committed to the path, we will play our own part in making more beauty and less suffering. John O'Donohue called beauty "the invisible embrace"; it's not naive to believe that beauty will save the world. It already has.

And it will go on saving the world as long as there are people who ask to be enfolded within this divine embrace and begin to take seriously the call to hold the space between the brokenness of the day and the perfection of the present moment. We don't know if this moment will last, but it is *our* moment, and we get to choose what to do with it.

For it is not reality that causes us to suffer but the stories we tell about it. Authentic, life-affirming spirituality does not deny the existence of violence, though it does surely work to transcend the negative effects of violence and to reduce the amount of violence in the world. It does this by helping human beings, one by one and in community, face our own shadows: our fears and wounds, the way we project evil onto "enemies," the temptation to smack down our opponents without considering the long-term health of people and the planet.

Growing through the struggle, the sorrow, and the repair underway in northern Ireland has shown me that the way to face the fear of the world is twofold, and both are about impact. We are here, partly, *to make an impact* on the world around us: to spend our lives in serving the common good, wherever we are called to be. To make a difference.

Even though the world we often see may not fully reveal itself in love, we each have within us an *unimpactable* core beneath the surface of our ego and personality and reputation and the external trappings of our lives. There's a task of discernment around the practices you can opt into that will grow the part of you that cannot be harmed, no matter what story other people are telling. Wise people call this part the true self. Wise people call this the act of truest storytelling: loving God and loving your neighbor as yourself.

Spiritual wisdom tells us that because of the unimpactable core, everything that matters is truly OK, even if they're crucifying you. That doesn't mean we shouldn't choose to be where we are most sheltered; it just means that we should not depend on external circumstances for our deepest sustenance. As humans, we have a job to do and an inheritance to claim. Part of our job is to have an impact on what we most fear, and part of it is to grow the unimpactable part of ourselves so that it becomes indistinguishable from the self we show to the world. Our *inheritance* is to do it in community: with other humans, with the ecosystem, with God. I used to think that because things were getting better, it was all right to feel OK. Now I tend to think that everything that matters most was always OK already, and the more people who believe that, the better things will get.

The northern Ireland story of conflict offers a warning of what happens when people believe the story of separation; the northern Ireland story of peacebuilding points to what's possible when we choose to risk a better story. Of course, there are many other times and places where such a transition was made. Perhaps you live in a place where amends for the wounds of conquest have not yet been made, where one type of person, gender, or ethnicity dominates others. Perhaps you live in a place where the Indigenous inhabitants were killed or violently diminished or where people were abducted in chains from somewhere far away in order to work the land. Perhaps the descendants of those Indigenous people and those people brought in chains are still suffering the injustice of inequality, where the abundant bounty of the land has been disproportionately kept from them. Perhaps you are one of those people who has been targeted. Or perhaps you are a descendant of the people who did the targeting. Perhaps, like me, your heritage includes a bit of both.

Whoever you are, the most important question you can ask now is about your gifts and needs. Whether or not you believe you earned the resources you hold—money, safety, power—the way to overcome the fear of the world is to use those resources for the common good. To make an impact for something beyond yourself. Whether or not you did anything to deserve the lack you feel—money, safety, power—the way to overcome the fear of the world is to find the part of you that cannot be destroyed even if they kill you. To grow the unimpactable part of yourself.

Authentic, life-affirming spirituality invites us to tell the truth about violence, which means sometimes facing painful realities but also getting things in proportion. We know that it is being widely argued that we currently live in the least violent time in human history. There is compelling evidence for this. Yet even if that argument is mistaken, or even if the reduction in violence is somehow reversed, we know that our spiritual evolution invites us to participate in the empowerment of women and historically excluded people, the expansion of democracy, the expansion of empathy, and the revolutions in human rights. Even if the trends change, the world becomes safer when courageous people tell a new story.

It's a story of connection, not separation; of creativity, not repetition of what didn't work before; of courageous action for the common good. It's a story in which we don't seek to avoid suffering and merely displace our suffering onto someone else but embrace a measure of suffering as an inevitable consequence of a life dedicated to the common good. It's a story that radically reorients our self-understanding, revealing that we are not individuals in competition with other individuals to get as much as we can and keep it for ourselves; instead, in this story, human beings are not the protagonists. The protagonist of this story is nothing less than Love: the willingness to stretch oneself for the sake of others. And the *purpose* of this story is nothing less than the triumph of Love over everything else.

This story leads its tellers to resist oppression and transcend it with a new way of being. They have chosen not to remain the victims of a story that says the world is only getting worse. And when the world is in trouble, they reject the story that says there is nothing we can do about it. Instead, they are the bringers of new light, the recipients of the gift of courage in the face of re-sistance, the bearers of the pain that is and the transcenders of the lie that exaggerates it, the initiators of what comes next on our journey toward wholeness. And they do this because they know just one thing.

There is a better story. Let's start telling it.

THE TASK BEFORE you may be to convert your fear of the world into a more truthful story. To reorient yourself beyond the surface of your circumstances and the story you're telling about them.

When you are afraid of the world, look at it sideways. Imagine how your life would be different had you been born in a different time or place. There were wars and plagues all the time, and there were no indoor toilets, and there was no re-corded music, and everyone's teeth were bad, and you couldn't get a cab anywhere! Imagine yourself into gratitude for the way your schooling and your playing and your working and your dreaming have been shaped by generations of people who loved you into being. And if that's not how it happened, or you can't find the thread of that story, know this: *you made it through those waters, and you're here.* Now.

Investigate not what you lack but the gift that has always lain behind the lack. It has waited for you, just until you were ready.

And when you look at the world through the dark prism of op-position, enmity, and rage—when it threatens to overwhelm, leav-ing you anxious that neither you nor the world will ever return to a place of calm—consider this: the good old days perhaps never were. You may remember them that way because you were being taken care of by hands that seemed invisible, and you had not seen what you have now. Was it the hands that changed or your story?

And even though you have memories of pain that is real, and even though there may even have been monsters that behaved monstrously, these truths remain.

There is a part of you that the monsters could not touch.

You are bigger than the monsters now.

Monsters are also people.

Your pain deserves attention, your wounds deserve to be bound, and your self deserves to be set free from a prison of despair and terror.

There is a seed of healing even within the wound.

Though you may know well the unwelcome racing of a damaged heart, you are not as weak as you think.

You have already been heroic just to get here. Just to get to now.

There may come a time when your wound is offered as a source of transformation even in the place where you were first harmed, to others who know the same wound, and even to those who have caused these wounds. But that may not be a task for today. Today may just be for you.

But when it's time, don't withhold your gift.

THE SIXTH WAY TO NOT BE AFRAID: GATHER AND DO THE WORK OF BELOVED COMMUNITY

IF THERE REALLY is a part of you that *cannot be impacted*, even by the things you fear the most, can you imagine the impact you could have on a broken and healing world?

Invite two friends for a cup of coffee. Take an hour together to imagine a way of being community that doesn't require leadership, expertise, or money but just time and an open heart. Imagine what the world could be like if everyone had a circle of six or seven good friends, each committed to their own journey of growth, each gaining clarity about their sense of purpose for the common good, each open to feedback from the others, and each different enough from each other that it doesn't get too repetitive.

I call these Porch Circles, as I like to invoke the idea of a relaxed conversation on a porch. I like this enough I even named a magazine *The Porch*. But you can call them whatever works for you. Porch Circles are a way to face the world together. They are a simple and accessible way of building community, discerning our needs and gifts, and sharing them for the sake of the common good. In other words, they help us grow both the unimpactable core of ourselves and the impact we can have on the world.

Back to the cup of coffee. Gather two friends—it's important that it be two and not one because a conversation between two people can often become a self-reinforcing loop. With three people, there is the possibility of community. The following questions are good for that journey. Share them with a handful of other humans on a regular basis. Combine this with putting on your seat belt, trying to avoid mosquitoes, and doing what you can to love God, your neighbor, the earth, and yourself. Then watch your fear shrink.

1. What is bringing you life?

2. What is challenging, draining, or deadening you?

3. We are awakening to the reality that there is no "them and us"; there is only us. In light of this, what is one opportunity you have had since we last met to live this story, and what did you do with that opportunity? (You could expand on this question. For instance, What did you learn from it? What would you like to do differently next time? What is an upcoming opportunity you know you will have to live this story, and what would you like to do with it?)

   After everyone has had the chance to respond to each of the three questions, ask the final question of the whole group:

4. Having heard what we have heard, is there anyone who would like to ask for something from the group, and is there anyone who would like to offer something to anyone in the group? This can be as practical as "I need a babysitter," as profound as "I am having an existential crisis and would like someone to go for a walk with me once a week for the next month," or as radical as "I can't pay my rent right now. Could the group help support me until I get on my feet?" At times of crisis, the need may be more urgent, and often the need will be for support with structural change or for an aspiring ally to step in to offer humble solidarity with folks who are directly burdened. But when burdens are shared in healthy interdependent community, they get lighter.

When you're finished, consider doing it again the following week. Over time, feel free to invite up to nine other folks (one at a time is best, and a maximum of twelve people allows for everyone to share their story meaningfully). Ask the same questions. See what happens. And do it again.

chapter 12

fear of
death

If I knew that tomorrow the world
would go to pieces,
I'd still plant my apple tree.

— Anonymous

THE FIRST TIME you died, you had been alive forever. You didn't know this at the time, but you had been living in a cave, surrounded by water so perfectly warm, it was always fine to swim in, and so perfectly balanced, you could even breathe it. It was a lovely cave.

Before the day came, you'd been in the cave for as long as you could remember. In fact, from the perspective you now inhabit, I'm not sure *remember* is an applicable term for the way you thought about the world. There was no past or future. You were just hanging out in the cave, defining the archetype of being cradled, periodically bouncing a little or kicking a lot, but for the most part sucking your thumb and ruling the universe. You were a benign ruler, of course; no concept of conflict or harm filled your mind, no Machiavellian textbooks on *How to Be a Bad Baby* found their way into the library of the particular womb you were enjoying. Innocence was not just all you knew but all you could conceive.

And then, an earthquake. The water you were breathing suddenly dispersed beneath you, a rushing silent whoosh being the last thing you didn't hear before you were squeezed down a tunnel that got narrower as you neared its exit. You didn't understand then what suffocating was, but you could certainly describe it now, your lungs coming under immediate and brutal pressure to exchange the amniotic fluid they had been breathing for the past nine months for the oxygen they would receive for the next whatever number of years. At the time, you didn't know what a lung *was*, never mind a *year*. But both were ready for you, entirely secure in their identity as years and lungs. You would have a breathing apparatus and time to use it. But you didn't need to think about that now. You were too busy being sent through the tunnel of doom, the walls collapsing inward like the trash compactor in *Star Wars*, the gunk of your prior eternity left behind, nothing to hold on to, an unstoppable roller coaster that apparently could only end with your destruction. You'd had a good ride, I suppose—a whole life consisting of nothing but having your needs met and sleeping, so complaining would have been churlish. Still, you were probably irritated. You had just gotten used to the cave, and now you were dying, unable to breathe, accelerating in anxiety toward who knows what.

This happened to me too. In the end, our first death was quick: a few mighty thrusts on the part of the cave builder, and we were expelled like a bank's pneumatic money tube, out into piercing light, revealing no warmth to our infant eyes. (We should note that for some of us, it was even quicker and more dramatic: the roof of the cave was suddenly torn open, and giant hands reached in to pull us out.) A being the size of Godzilla picked us up, slapped us on our backsides, and with a pair of scissors almost as big as we were, cut the cord that connected us to all we had ever known. It was cold and dry and lonely, and we were surrounded by giants.

You bet we cried.

———————————

BUT IT TURNED out OK in the end. Or in the beginning. Because when I consider just how confused I used to be about something as personal as my own birth—how completely I had misread this universal miracle—I'm hesitant to make absolute assertions about the thing I'm experiencing now, the bit they call "life." I'm more than halfway through the traditionally mandated threescore years and ten, but when I consider the category error I made in interpreting my own birth as the *beginning* of the only life I'll have rather than as the *end* of a previous one, I'm not sure beginnings and endings are what we suppose them to be.

The breathtaking, breath-giving result of reimagining your birth as the end of something is twofold. The first is the humility before nature and the transcendent that we have discussed earlier—that is, if you can't *understand* everything, then you don't have to worry about *controlling* it all. It takes some of us quite a while before we recognize this as a blessing; some of us never do, and we rage against the possibility that some things are not our business. There is a reason the invocation that has served millions of folks seeking recovery from alcohol dependency and other addictions is called the Serenity Prayer, because accepting the things I cannot change actually does open up a space in which the heart can become at peace. This may be one reason the tradition perhaps most committed to such acceptance has produced a leader in the form of the fourteenth Dalai Lama, who has focused more on the well-being of the human heart than on traditional political activism, believing that more whole hearts make more effective activists. Whatever may be true for him, the first gift of reimagining your birth as a kind of death is to return again to the time when you were utterly secure. Even unconscious of the existence of threats to your sense of security, arriving at a place where, as my friend Jim Harrison put it, "it does not even occur to you to feel fear."

The second gift of reimagining your birth is the most wonderful surprise, and if you ponder it for a lifetime or a second, it can become the key to the gentle undermining of all fear. You see, I think that the root of all fear is the fear of death. We slice into our skin and pull it back to defy the effects of aging, forgetting that elders should be honored as anchors for the community to learn how to be. We plug metal and plastic and computers into our veins to keep the body alive long after the spirit has begun to wander elsewhere. In our worst moments, we allow others to die through our inaction—or sometimes even violently take their lives—because we have come to believe the demonic lie that the power to kill equates to the power over death itself.

Our culture is terrified of dying. We don't know how to do it well. In Western culture, we bury the dead quickly, and we call funerals "celebrations," as if we can't face the notion that in some very real sense, the person we loved is actually gone. And at the back of each of our minds is a gnawing voice that tries to trap us into thinking that the fact that we will all eventually die means that everything else is meaningless. And so we may feel that we must do everything we can to fend off the moment when the body will set us free. We imprison ourselves in the worldview that says the worst and most important thing that will happen to us is that we will die.

We often measure life by death. When someone close to home dies, we remember the times we shared with them or moments when they happened to be present; it helps us measure our own years and perhaps deepens our sense of wanting to live better. There was a time when I refrained from reading news websites because they stirred up unnecessary fear, delusions of grandeur, and wasted time. But news still leaked through, and

I still heard about the deaths of celebrities. It was notable how many people would tell me when public figures passed away, and I heard more about the famous newly dead than about war or politics.

And of course, there *is* a time to celebrate the lives of those who have gone before. Not long before I began writing this book, Lakota educator and activist Richard Twiss suddenly died.* My mourning was tempered by the memory of the last time I had seen him, when he blessed the closing of a retreat with sage. As I understand them, his traditions hold that there should be up to a year of mourning before the celebration of the person's life can begin. I felt that the sage blessing had become Richard's farewell to some of us, and after a year had passed, it was now more in tune with the emotional terrain to celebrate his life. If helping people die is one of the greatest privileges of the spiritual path, then helping the bereaved integrate the loss may be the next.

The lovely ideas that Elisabeth Kübler-Ross proposed for understanding the stages of dying and grief are resonant with all kinds of experiences of letting go. While the stages can happen in various orders and overlap, the first stage is often denial, followed by anger, depression, bargaining, and then the joy—or the peace or even the glory—of acceptance. When we conceive of death as the end of everything, it's easy to want to deny it. If we travel that path, the next stage will be to indulge anger at the apparent injustice of death, to be brought into this difficult world just to suffer and die! Fight that battle for a little while and you'll tire yourself out, and that exhausted vacuum will be filled with melancholia. Such bleakness, thankfully, can't snap at your heels forever, and once it has tired of that, the old belief that you can control destiny will find its way back. Then you

---

* I'm thankful that we have Richard's books to learn from: *One Church, Many Tribes* and *Rescuing the Gospel from the Cowboys: A Native American Expression of the Jesus Way.*

might try to negotiate with the doors of perception, asking them only to open part of the way, but sometimes telling revelation to censor itself can be like thinking you can stop the tide by blowing on it. The bargain with death may involve plastic and metal and computers, or artificially reshaping your face to look younger, or confusing childishness with wonder. And then, if you allow the light in, acceptance. Not fighting anymore. Serenity.

The body does not often feel ready to accept the death of loved ones, especially when those deaths happen suddenly. We sometimes need generous friends to help us through the stages of grief, and perhaps this journey needs to last for as long as we are here. Grief and joy will always coexist. But I want to suggest that there is a story that will not only assist with your own grieving but help make you into the kind of person to whom others flock when they need comfort. More than that, this story can help us integrate all our fears, lessen the debilitating power they have over us, and even let them turn into sources of excitement, joy, and, yes, more life.

All fears are rooted in the fear of death, yet the fear of death is based on a huge misunderstanding. There was a time when you were more secure and more loved and more the source of other people's hopes than you could possibly have known. And then something happened that left you thinking it was all over. That was the miracle of your own birth.

I like to think that what we call "life" is nothing less than a more conscious version of our gestation in the womb. We are not as alone as we think we are. The universe is our womb now. And we have no idea what happens when the body dies.

Except maybe we do. We know that many people have reported near-death experiences, during which they felt they were traveling down a tunnel toward a light. We know that the memories of dead loved ones often seem more real than the thoughts we have of living friends. The existence of a soul that goes on after the body has decayed is not verifiable by science as currently understood. Atheists can't prove the soul does *not* exist any more than religious dogma can prove it *does*.

Whether you think the soul exists may not really matter in the end, because what the soul actually does is *insist*. It is *there*, and it is a mystery. Serenity comes from accepting the mystery of the soul's insistence.

SO THE MOST frightening and insecure thing that could ever happen to you has already occurred. You couldn't have been here without it. You would have no consciousness—no likes or dislikes, no knowledge, no presence—if it hadn't taken place. The greatest shelter from fear a human being can know is intrinsic to how we were designed, and it is simply this: nothing more insecure than your own birth can ever happen to you. Your own birth was merely the first miracle in a life that is partly an unfolding of obstacles for the purpose of your own growth, partly a scavenger hunt in which you get to be surprised by the ecstasy of finding treasure, partly a garden for you to tend for the sake of life itself. That garden contains edible flowers and poison ivy alike. So tending it is a heroic quest with enormous struggle and cosmic delight, with no end higher than the discovery that the Grail is you.

Birth happens. Things fall apart. Things collapse: sometimes people, sometimes cities, sometimes the stories we tell about them. There is renewal and rebuilding and the building of something new. Death is most assuredly not the end.

Helping someone die is one of the most sacred privileges of service. What a gift: to accompany someone as they begin to transition, perhaps reimagining their lives, saying farewell to loved ones, getting ready to walk over the bridge you're helping them build. Being present at the good death of another will reduce your own fear of death and increase the sense of peaceful mystery that surrounds this inevitability.

Jesuit priest and psychotherapist Anthony de Mello used to invite people into a guided meditation on the stages of decay that their own corpse would eventually experience. If you're new to this, it might seem almost laughable to think that such an exercise would be appropriate for contemplation. But this is strong medicine for a strong sickness. For if our fears are so deeply connected to our dissociation from the body, then we will be well served by anything we can do to reconnect with our flesh. At the risk of sounding morbid, another gift would be to imagine all the benefits of death: no responsibilities, nothing to worry about, no sense of lack (not to mention all the love that is poured out when people miss you).

We don't have to *seek* death. But if all we do is *fear* it, it will be as if it has already happened, and not for our good. Our own death can be premature and incomplete if we don't learn to face it while we have the conscious capacity. There are life-enhancing properties in being aware of our own death. It helps us see life as an in-between space rather than all there is. It helps us savor the moment, or the day, or the year. It helps us accept the many little deaths that come our way in life: think of friendships that now only exist in memory, or tasks completed, or things that didn't work out the way we expected. It also helps us conceive of little resurrections: when the unexpected thing turned out to be magnificent, when a new path opened up that seemed impossible, when we recovered from a sorrow or an illness.

So in a certain sense, what we call life is at least partly a preparation for death, and death is what some traditions call a "giveaway." The people who will mourn you will be doing so because of the gift you gave them. The manner of your dying will be part of that gift, just as the manner of your living will be shaped by your perception of death.

My maternal grandparents died an hour apart. She at seventy-three, he at eighty-three, they gave each other the gift of neither having to grieve their loss.

A few days before the effects of dementia overcame his body, I helped bathe my mentor, Walter, him lying naked and frail, like a pietà Jesus, in a light-filled room with his wife, June, and his nurse and his friend. Walter had dedicated his working life to educating people about domination and the power structures of this world. In his dying, he embodied giving up domination.

The truth of the carpenter from Nazareth—that all laws find their fulfillment in love—will never die, partly because of the way he did. The momentary power of the state and religious authorities cannot outlast the nonviolent acceptance of physical death overcome by a better story. Love cannot be killed.

Your first death has already helped heal people, and it can do that for you too. Your birth was immensely risky and even more unlikely—just think about the few happenings out of billions of possibilities that needed to collide for your conception to occur! The Herculean journey to get here! Your first death brought you into the world of stories, and one true story, I'm confident, is that you have had an untold impact in the lives of others. I promise you, no matter how low an opinion you may have of your life thus far, the very fact of your birth is enough to awaken hope in the hearts of people living with the burden of fear.

It is not too late to choose a conscious life, attending to the practices that call forth the true self. You are not far from the true self. In fact, you couldn't be nearer. All that stands between your surface self and your true self is memory and will. Are you willing to remember that there is a core beneath the core of who you think you are and to choose to open to it? If you do that, the healing of others will continue simply because they are near you. It will not necessarily be easy. But it is simpler than you may think.

THE ORIGINAL TITLE for this book was *Seeing in the Dark*. On the news, in TV and movies, and in our fearful minds, the dark is where bad things happen. This results from a sometimes deadly mingling of superstition, confirmation bias, a bit of data, and amygdalae running riot, pulling the wool over our better senses.

Of course bad things happen in the dark, because it's easy to hide things there. But bad things happen in the light too. Decisions made at tables in skylighted boardrooms, conversations held behind "respectable" white picket fences: these too are subject to the self-dealing tendencies of human corruption. Just as Shakespeare's Richard III "can smile, and murder whiles I smile," we all know the term *daylight robbery*.

The fourteenth Dalai Lama is quoted as saying that the best thing Americans (and presumably, anyone in an industrial society) can do to live better is to go to bed when it gets dark and wake up when it's getting light. Light and shadow each bring distinct gifts, and if we don't learn to receive them and to work with them, we might miss life itself.

So the dark may be a little scary at times, but wondrous things happen there too: fireflies and lovemaking, carol singing and candle lighting, campfire storytelling and cinema, life-renewing hibernation, an irreplaceable motion in the rhythm of life.

Beyond that, I'm taken with Virginia Woolf's notion, foregrounded by Rebecca Solnit in her book *Hope in the Dark*, that "the dark" is not necessarily bad or good; it's just *dark*. By its very nature, we can't "see" it. Deeper still, in the realm of myth, the dark is where things that could never happen elsewhere are actually possible. I once heard Irish shaman John Moriarty tell a story of one night seeing the moonlit ocean through his window as he crossed the pitch-dark room to switch on an electric light. The beauty of what he witnessed—light from an astronomical body illuminating the water—was ineffable. But when he switched on the electric light inside the room, the beauty disappeared. He could no longer see the ocean when the light was on. So he switched it off again and stared at the moonlit deep for hours, drinking in the light that could only be seen in the dark.

That some things can only be found in the dark, in the not-knowing, is a revealing and even transformative truth. And the warm good news is that the dark is already our friend. We are invited to go forward by *returning* because darkness was the first thing we knew.

I once had a nightmare that I was being chased down the street by a monstrous figure with a horrifying weapon who was intent on annihilating me. We were both running faster than I felt able, and he kept trying to grab my shoulder to spin me around and kill me. Just at the second he finally got hold of my shoulder, I woke up screaming. Brian had his hand on the center of my back, trying to gently wake me. Having himself been awakened by my cries, he wanted to get me out of the bad dream.

"You're OK. You're OK," he said, tender, confident. "You have what you need."

By then I knew enough about how the body retains and re-solves trauma to slow down my breathing. So I lay there awake for quite some time, consciously inhaling and exhaling at a pace that would regulate my heart rate and enable me to re-arrange the disturbed furniture of my mind.

The next day, I pondered the dream. It seemed to me that the man who was trying to kill me represented something like the twin spirits of nihilism and despair, which have so often snatched at my mind when I'm awake. You may feel the same way sometimes: the sense that life is meaningless or that there is so much pain in the world that we are triggered into unbearable hopelessness. That's a very ordinary feeling. As with so much in the realm touched by fear, that itself is the first good news. If such emotions are common, then none of us is alone.

But there's even better news.

Another night I had a different dream, and this time I woke up laughing. It was a simple dream about something that really happened to me in 1986. In the dream, I was eleven years old and walking down a street, listening to music through what I called a "Walkman" but was a generic knockoff, much less expensive than the official Sony-branded model. The song was "The Power of Love" by Huey Lewis and the News. You may not previously have considered this song to be a profound psychological work, but pay attention and you may find at its heart a fair bit of wisdom. Huey—and indeed, the News also—wants us to know that love is free but costly, comes out of nowhere yet is seemingly everywhere, can overwhelm us, and can stimulate great pain, but if we give ourselves to it, what else could we possibly want or need?

I woke up dreaming the middle of the song, and I really was laughing. Because the feeling I had in my chest, listening to that song at eleven years old—the feeling of exhilaration, of possibility, of utter *okayness* with the world, or at least with whatever was happening in that particular moment—was suddenly flooding my forty-two-year-old mind as if it had never left. And it had left, you see, because I had made too many mistakes and taken on too many burdens to hold on to joy.

Anyway, innocence has to grow up before it can become wonder. And here I was with the very feeling I had known in my chest decades ago, with wonder enveloping me in a dream.

And I realized, everything that happens occurs in my mind. The perception I have of the world is all I have to go on. And I can consciously choose which lens to wear. The twin spirits of nihilism and despair exist *in my mind*; the spirit of innocence evolving into wonder exists *in my mind too*. I can choose what to do with my mind. Just as the body keeps the score of the worst things that have happened to us, so it also retains the happiest! All the joys and hopes and passions and smiles and anticipations and glorious becomings that you have experienced still exist in your body. They are just waiting for you to remember them and to choose the ways that will bridge the gap between what your ego thinks it wants and what your true self could never lose.

The current global crisis is a crisis of storytelling. Tell the story in a way that exaggerates fear, and violence will increase. Tell the story in a way that decreases fear, and violence will reduce.

We can transform our fear by the stories we tell.

We have a better story. It started when your first death gave you life.

THE SEVENTH WAY TO NOT BE AFRAID: ASK WHAT YOU CAN SEE IN THE DARK

WHAT'S OFTEN MOST frightening is not the thing we believe will happen but the uncertainty of what *might*. Facing uncertainty is what is required to be in the world at any given moment. This might seem to be bad news: we will never escape from anxiety, whether background or dramatic.

But there's another way of seeing it: If uncertainty is a permanent fact of life, what if we stopped trying to fight it? What if we stopped playing the game—the game of trying to control the future or what people think of us or might do to us—altogether?

What if we started to live as if we were already dead? Not zombies staggering around with nowhere to go or martyrs traumatized through persecution but those awake to what really matters because they no longer care about what doesn't.

What's most real is what's *inside*, and it may well have been there long before you ever noticed it. You can ignore it, but you can't erase it. You can befriend it—or better still, let it befriend you. It can offer reassurance that you are just fine. You always were. You're not here to "succeed" or to expand your territory. You're here to die to everything that does not honor reality, to everything that does not give life.

Before we can ever truly experience the moment we're living in, we need to forgo the fake comfort of false certainty about the future. Recognizing that we wouldn't be here at all if we had not surrendered to our first death will not only help us prepare for our second—whenever that may come—but can help us figure out what really matters today. And what doesn't matter at all.

So a final invitation presents itself.

Would you consider entering the darkness not of terror but of not knowing?

Would you begin by closing your eyes or even switching off the light and giving just an hour to asking yourself the question "What can I see in the dark?"

epilogue

HOW DO WE make peace in a world where domination is often portrayed as not only respectable but sacred? How can we live as families and communities when social structures often seem to be doing everything they can to undermine bonds of interdependence and kindness? How can we build friendships when there is no time? How can we afford to relax when so many of us are afraid of not having enough money? How can we heal the epidemic of depression that seems to spread like an airborne virus, no matter where in the world we happen to be? How can we overcome the paralyzing consequences of being terrified of what other people might do to us? How can we even get through a day when we're bombarded by stories of gigantic danger, which may directly threaten us? How, ultimately, can we find peace with our gods and each other and, eventually, look at ourselves in the mirror and smile?

I have come to believe that what I need is simple:

> I need a close circle of about a dozen people—each of whom is emotionally mature in ways that the rest of us aren't—with whom to find support, encouragement, celebration, mourning, and dancing.
>
> I need initiation by elders and continued mentoring into balancing the archetypal parts of my being: the lover, the sovereign, the warrior-protector, and the magician.

I need to discern a sense of purpose grounded in my true self, seeing the privileges I inhabit as a resource from which to serve the common good and my lack as a place from which to invite solidarity.

I need to devote my attention to beauty more often than suffering. For it is beauty that will lead us to step into a world in which there is always more than enough of what we need or could ever want.

I need to breathe a little more slowly.

THE WORLD IS not falling apart. But the story we're telling about it could use some help.

Here are a few steps you might take.

1. Thanks for reading this book. Consider going back to the beginning, responding to the invitations in part 1, and trying the ways at the end of each chapter in part 2, perhaps practicing the same one daily for an entire week before moving to the next.

2. At the very end of the book is a series of "Blessings," offered in the sacred tradition of invoking healing, protection, or action. You might read them aloud, one at a time on specific occasions of need, or all together when you want to reset your relationship with fear.

3. When you encounter a story, ask yourself, "Is the story true, and is it helpful?" If the answer is no for either, take responsibility for finding—or making—a truer or more helpful version.

4. Commit to learning to consciously take hold of your relationship with electronic communication, social media, the news, and popular culture rather than letting them run you.

5. Spend more time with friends than machines.

6. Consider forming a Porch Circle, where groups of three to twelve people share life together. (More details at the end of

chapter 11 and here: https://www.theporchmagazine.com/ porch-circles.)

7. Breathe.
8. Consider spending one week each quarter going to bed when it gets dark and getting up when it's light.
9. Ask yourself what you have and how you can share it to serve the common good. Ask yourself what you lack and who are the safe people from whom you can ask for help.
10. If you have found them helpful, share the ideas in this book with others.

We're not here to *conquer* our fears, but we can *transform* them through a story in which fear finds its proper place. Learning that story is a lifelong journey, whose terrain includes both mountain tops and stumbling blocks.

One of those stumbling blocks is the fear that we will never change. If that's a familiar thought, know this: all spiritual wisdom traditions agree that no matter how yesterday went, you can rejoin the path today.

Nothing that has gone before is wasted: your own mistakes and those made by others, the wounds that have yet to become scars and the ones that have already turned into superpowers, the agonized prayers and celebratory dances, the night terrors, the daytime anxiety, the desire to help, the hope for a better world, and the commitment to play your part in it. All of these blessings and all of these burdens can be harvested, for the good, through the stories we tell. Even the demons can be healed. The makings of a better story are already within us. All we need to do is befriend them.

So let's begin.

blessings

A Blessing for Not Being Alone

When watching a winter river flow,
the eddy and curl,
the jag of ice in the middle,
the snow banked on two sides,
the rocks,
the breezing branches of the looming pine,
the fallen branches beside them,
May you see everything that there is to see.

May you know that only you see it this way, this now.

This river, this eddy and curl, this bit of ice, and the snow,
the rocks, the branches: *You're their witness.*

May you come to know, in the deepest place,
the reality of friendship.
The friendship of reality.

The universe, full with open hands beckoning.
Waiting.
For you to befriend it.

A Blessing for Breath

Breathe,
knowing that every molecule
both within and without your body is stardust
and imbued with the light of God—
nothing separate, all a spiral into and from Love.

Breathe,
knowing that the worst pain in your life
has already been experienced by the mercy of the universe.

Breathe,
knowing that if the stones yearn to become cathedrals,
then you—enfleshment of divinity, mingling of sacred and
    profane,
a little lower than the angels—
are not the sum total of the worst things that have
    happened to you
or the worst things you have done.

Breathe,
knowing that the ones you admire the most—
the Gandhis and Mother Teresas and Fannie Lou Hamers
    and those who clear land mines and lie down with
    lions for the sake of peace—
these are the fruits of lives that have been crucibled in
    suffering.
No one becomes great without first being brought low.
No one develops true empathy for the greatest suffering
without touching some of that suffering themselves.

Breathe.

A Blessing for Discovering That the Ordinary Is Always Extraordinary

When the morning comes, may you wake up,
letting your grip on the night slip away, and turn over to
greet yourself.

It's a new day,
and you are here.

There is no less love on this day than there was on your
best, no fewer opportunities to make more love.

The crystal exfoliation of water on the skin,
the shiny green freshness of the apple in the fruit bowl,
the zero gravity of feet on the ground, eyes closed, thankful.

The transcendental space occupied by the first and the
next and the last persons you see.

The heart in the music you will hear.

May you come to experience the deep knowing that the
purpose of time is to show you are alive—and so may
you come no longer to be dominated by but to dance
with time.

May you come to know your life's work—and so may you
enjoy the mingling of mission with work and play.

May you hear the inner voice of meaning—
and thus may you come to own your story so that you can
write the ending.

A BLESSING OF ENOUGH

May you come to see that you are enfolded into the God
    who laughs,
your place in the universe is assured,
and you are limited only by the story you are telling
    yourself.

It is said that those who own their story get to benefit
        from it and can become healing agents amid the
        darkness of shame and fear.
Owning the story means owning time.
Owning time makes you capable of miracles.

May you learn to own your story so that you can heal
    yourself.

A BLESSING FOR WHEN
THE WORLD SEEMS TOO MUCH

You are light.
You are holy.
You are called.
Into this moment. This time and place.
Invisible hands hold you.
You are not cursed.
You are called.
You have made it this far, and now is not the time to
    start fighting against reality.
Some folks didn't make it this far.
May we do for them what they are no longer able
    to do.
Live.

A Blessing for the Next Step

It's no wonder you want to be a peacemaker,
for you have seen so much conflict.

It's no wonder you want to heal shame,
for you have been a home for humiliation.

It's no wonder that you have sat in the ashes of loneliness,
for you have been scapegoated to the point of wanting to die.

It's no wonder that you want to transform supremacist stories,
    scapegoating stories, selfish stories, separation stories,
for you know the weight of what happens when humans do
    not do their inner work.

So

May you go to places of most delighted knowing with
    friends and deepest intimacy with lovers and through
    the dangerous, exhilarating woods of activism with
    comrades.

May you emerge into spacious places, finding reassurance
    that you did not deserve to be burdened by other
    people's shadows.

May you discover that poisonous shame is built on a lie
    and your loneliness is not the end.

May you find the path to honest amends for your mistakes
    and repair for the hurt you have known.
As the pain is healed and the gifts come into bloom, may
    they dance with each other.

May the fruit of kindness and solidarity be full on
     your lips.
And may you discover, and carefully hold, a vision
     of what you're here for.

Brilliantly creative,
courage when you need it,
with all the community you need,
woven into the fabric of this moment's crisis,
and this moment's gift.

A sovereign,
a lover,
a magician,
a warrior-protector
for the common good.

May your wound transform
first into a scar,
and then
a medicine story.

A Blessing for Seeing in the Dark

No one can know your darkness like you can.
And even you will not *know* it unless you *face* it.
Strange, I know, to imagine *facing* something you
     cannot see.

But there are things that can only be found in the dark.
There is light that can only be seen in the dark.
There may even be fragments or dimensions of love that
     will only touch you if you let them visit you in the dark.

You are here not just to save the world but to be changed.

So may nighttime bring you in touch with memory—an
    examen of the day, with gratitude and learning; of
    the year; of your life and the seven generations that
    brought you here.
And with possibility—of the year, of your life and the
    seven generations to come.

May you wake from your dreams laughing,
and carry innocence-becoming-wonder wherever you go.

May you tread lightly on the earth.
Know that she belongs to you,
and in her is your belonging too.

A Blessing for Friendship with Your Own Soul

You deserve to be known by the miracle of a day.
You are cradled through the night, the dusk affirming
    yesterday's work.
You don't just wake. You awaken unto something.

Stand in front of the mirror and repeat twenty times,
"I'm supercool, and beautiful, and thrillingly alive."
In the shower, be gentle with your skin, as if you were
    caressing a Rodin sculpture.
Pick up the first piece of trash you see and turn it into an
    origami Yoda.
Make breakfast as if you were making love, and eat it that
    way too.
Make sure no one's looking.

This time is for you.
To ready yourself for the miracle of a day.
Your day.

Go out into the world of wonder—trees and cars and
    roads and buildings and books and restaurants
    and computers and desks and the greatest
    wonder: people!
Oh, people, messed up and gorgeous, alive and dying,
    deceitful and trying, and trying hard to be good.

They need you.
We need you.

Hold yourself like you believe in your own glory—not
    more than or less than others, but inviting them into
    the same.

Stretch your arms and legs and neck and let your voice
    transcend Whitman, for goodness' sake: make it a
    beatific yawp!
Take yourself out to lunch and enjoy the sacrament
    of interruption that is queuing and choosing
    and eating.

Look up at the sky!
This is your roof.
Know that you're not the only one thinking this.
And that both of you are right.

Then when the working day is winding down,
readying itself to give way to rest and play,
find someone who needs your smile.
Give it to them. And you'll never lose it.

May you find the *Anam Cara* within.
Soul friendship with yourself,
that opens unto others,
makes a home for them,
and transfigures your inner life.

May you be the friend to yourself that we are all
  waiting for.

acknowledgments

THE GENEROSITY OF friends and colleagues made this book part of my relationships, in some cases for years. I thank them for showing up in my life when they did and for staying as long as they have.

Countless friends gave input, and it's impossible to name them all. Along with the beloved communities of Circle of Mercy, the Mankind Project, Movies & Meaning, *The Porch*, and the New Story Festival, as well as my family, each of the following people gave me particular encouragement, feedback, and affirmation to stay the course.

My partner in life and beautiful work together, Brian Ammons; my *better* teacher, Melvin Bray; my writing group partners Giles Carwyn and Pana Columbus; my New Story co-conspirator, Mike Clawson; the brilliant maker of both films and breakfasts, Mark Cousins; my supportive agent, Greg Daniel; the lateral thinker and pastoral genius Steve Daugherty; my dear friend and the very definition of a Renaissance man, Rodrigo Dorfman; my Soul Telegram collaborator, Cathleen Falsani; the wonderful Maranu Gascoigne; the calm and courageous Tyrone Greenlee; the magnificent Wendy Grisham; the eminent Lyndon Harris; Kathy Helmers, who was there at the start; poet and provocateur of peace Paul Hutchinson;

justice doula Micky ScottBey Jones; humble activist Steve Roach Knight; Dave Krysko, who is generous with ideas and hospitality; David LaMotte, who waited five years for me to respond to his feedback; the marvelous conflict transformer Michelle LeBaron; the shockingly good dancer Geoff Little; my colleague in the conversation that never ends, Jett Loe; David MacDonald, who taught me to breathe more slowly; Daniel Maldonado, who saw things in me I wasn't ready to see for myself; peaceful warrior and documentary maker Frederick Marx; Vincent Matthew Edralin, who mirrors self-acceptance so powerfully; Tyler McCabe, who supported the writing, in his words, "for the sheer humanitarian thrill of it!"; the sometimes bearded and always hilarious Carl McColman; the extraordinary poet Gail McConnell; the most generous coauthor, Brian McLaren; legendary roommate Richard Moor; my favorite spiritual director, Karen Moore; our true neighbors in all respects, Mike Morrell and Jasmin Pittman Morrell; my movie buddy, Kathleen Norris; Gabriel Peltier, who changed my life; the wise and always hilarious Nance Pettit; Jacob Ratliff, who does everything I can't; my home away from home, Mike and Rosemary Riddell; swami Nicholaes Roosevelt; Guy Sayles, with whom I shared the best laughter in years; Frank Schaeffer, who is always there when I ask; my pastor, Nancy Hastings Sehested; my true comrade, Mark Silver; Valerie Weaver-Zercher, who edited this book with grace, patience, and clarity; my Medicine Stories ally, David Wilcox; and friends whose acceptance and belonging are always gifts: Tom and Anne Butler, Michael Dowd, K. Stellar Dutcher, Eric Elnes, James Mcleary, Dan Mermin, Danny Morris, James Navé, Will "Shuggy" Otto, Michael Poffenberger, Drew Potter, Linda Sack, Don Shriver and Peggy Leu Shriver, Kristine Socall, Dan Snyder, Chance Taureau, Barry Taylor, Scott Teems, Vic Thiessen, Tim Tyson, George Viney, Jared Williams, June Keener Wink, and Colin Fraser Wishart.

Many of these people are writers, musicians, artists, teachers, and activists—I invite you to look for their life-giving work.

Ultimately, what these good people's names remind me is that there is no more spacious home than friendship. All of these friends are brilliant, like the rest of us. It is good to remember this, and often.

notes

xvi **"Whether things are getting better or worse depends on the vantage point and the measures of what concerns us."** On the relevant concepts of the "Great Unraveling" and the "Great Turning," see Joanna Macy and Molly Brown, *Coming Back to Life: The Updated Guide to the Work That Reconnects* (Gabriola Island, British Columbia: New Society, 2014).

xvii **"Where we are born into privilege"** adrienne maree brown, "Report: Recommendations for Us Right Now from a Future," *Sublevel Mag*, November 26, 2019, https://tinyurl.com/y6yfpudm.

2 **"dropping slow"** W. B. Yeats, "The Lake Isle of Innisfree," in *The Collected Poems of W. B. Yeats* (London: Palgrave Macmillan, 1989).

9 **"It's also worth noting that the root words"** Peter Kingsley, *Catafalque* (London: Catafalque, 2018).

11 **"Indeed, the current moment has stirred anxiety in profound ways"** The psychologist Abigail Marsh offers two helpful steps for managing fear during the coronavirus pandemic that are applicable to the necessary and legitimate fears in everyday life:

"Seeking good information" (which for our purposes must include *wisdom* as well as *facts*) and "sensible exposure to the threat." See Abigail Marsh, "How We Can Keep Fear from Spiraling Out of Control," *Washington Post*, June 23, 2020, https://tinyurl.com/managingnecessaryfear.

CHAPTER 1: WHAT ARE YOU AFRAID OF?

17 *"The average human is living in arguably the most peaceable time"* See Steven Pinker, *The Better Angels of Our Nature: Why Violence Has Declined* (New York: Penguin, 2012).

23 *"First, find a quiet place to sit"* This exercise, learned in therapy, is modeled on the HeartMath Quick Coherence Technique: https://tinyurl.com/y3emkdjl.

CHAPTER 2: FEAR IS A STORY

30 *"In his poem 'The Skylight'"* Seamus Heaney, "The Skylight," in *Seeing Things* (London: Faber and Faber, 1991).

32 *"Spirituality is our living relationship with mystery"* Steven Sundborg, quoted by Thomas Hart, *Spiritual Quest: A Guide to the Changing Landscape* (Mahwah, NJ: Paulist, 1999), 40.

33 *"Most of us are living in a more peaceable world than ever."* For comprehensive evidence and arguments in this direction, see Pinker's *Better Angels of Our Nature*; Hans Rosling, Anna Rosling Rönnlund, and Ola Rosling's *Factfulness: Ten Reasons We're Wrong about the World—and Why Things Are Better Than You Think* (New York: Flatiron, 2018); and the constantly updated website http://www.humanprogress.org.

33 *"But the expanding circle of empathy sensitizes us to pain"* See Peter Singer, *The Expanding Circle: Ethics, Evolution, and Moral Progress* (Princeton, NJ: Princeton University Press, 2011).

33 *"Rates of violence are likely linked to social inequality"* Eric Michael Johnson, "The Joker's Wild: On the Ecology of Gun

Violence in America," *Scientific American*, July 26, 2012, https://tinyurl.com/y37qr6vc.

33 ***"Bombing instead of talking to our enemies"*** See Erica Chenoweth and Maria J. Stephan, *Why Civil Resistance Works: The Strategic Logic of Nonviolent Conflict* (New York: Columbia University Press, 2012).

34 ***"The best criticism of the bad is the practice of the better"*** Richard Rohr, "The Eight Core Principles of the Center for Action and Contemplation," Center for Action and Contemplation, https://tinyurl.com/y532vmrm.

35 ***"Don't be afraid of anyone."*** Laurie Anderson's speech on behalf of Lou Reed at the 2015 Rock 'n' Roll Hall of Fame induction ceremony; more details here: https://tinyurl.com/LaurieLou.

36 ***"The best way I have found to describe this is that we find our place"*** See Gareth Higgins and Brian McLaren, *The Seventh Story: Us, Them, and the End of Violence* (Asheville, NC: The Porch, 2018).

Chapter 3: A Brief History of Fear

43 ***"Human-eating predators, the poet naturalist David Quammen tells us"*** David Quammen, *Monster of God: The Man-Eating Predator in the Jungles of History and the Mind* (New York: W. W. Norton, 2003).

45 ***"We've all observed what theologian and biblical scholar Walter Wink calls the 'domination system'"*** For the most accessible introduction to Walter Wink's epochally important work, see *The Powers That Be: Theology for a New Millennium* (New York: Harmony, 1999).

48 ***"This means giving away what Simone Weil called our greatest power"*** Simone Weil, *Gravity and Grace* (London: Routledge & Kegan Paul, 1952).

54 ***"There's a Hopi invocation that"*** Hopi elders prophecy, "We Are the Ones We've Been Waiting For," Awakin.org, June 8, 2000, https://tinyurl.com/hopielders.

55 **"Brian McLaren defines ritual as"** Brian McLaren, *Why Did Jesus, Moses, the Buddha, and Mohammed Cross the Road? Christian Identity in a Multi-faith World* (Nashville: Jericho Books, 2012).

Chapter 4: You Don't Know the End of the Story

59 **"whatever you say, say nothing."** Seamus Heaney, "Whatever You Say, Say Nothing," in *North* (London: Faber and Faber, 1975).

61 **"For the story played by Ingrid Bergman and Humphrey Bogart"** I'm indebted to screenwriting teacher Robert McKee for this interpretation of *Casablanca*. I heard him talk about it at a seminar; http://www.mckeestory.com.

Chapter 5: Your Story Can Be a Shelter

71 **"the mirror, enshrining the ugly"** John O'Donohue, *Beauty: The Invisible Embrace* (New York: Harper Perennial, 2005).

74 **"the eye with which I see God"** Meister Eckhart, *The Complete Mystical Works of Meister Eckhart*, trans. Maurice O'C. Walshe (Freiburg im Breisgau, Germany: Herder & Herder, 2010).

75 **"Holy wells sometimes became sites of political resistance"** Michael P. Carroll, *Irish Pilgrimage: Holy Wells and Popular Catholic Devotion* (Baltimore: Johns Hopkins University Press, 1999).

Chapter 6: Fear of Being Alone

84 **"In Autobiography of Red, the poet Anne Carson describes"** Anne Carson, *Autobiography of Red* (New York: Alfred A. Knopf, 1998).

88 **"The essential religious experience is that you are being known"** Richard Rohr, *The Naked Now: Learning to See as the Mystics See* (Chestnut Ridge, NY: Crossroad, 1999).

89 **"We are not alone, we live in God's world."** United Church of Canada, "A New Creed," 1968; rev. 1980, 1995, https://tinyurl.com/y2eq3b2b.

Chapter 7: Fear of Having Done Something That Can't Be Fixed

97 *"Counseling sessions failed when I broke the chair I sat on"* This poem is unpublished at the time of this writing, but you can find more of the poet's work in Paul Hutchinson, *Between the Bells: Stories of Reconciliation from Corrymeela* (Norwich, UK: Canterbury, 2019).

Chapter 8: Fear of a Meaningless Life

112 *"A great artist is never poor."* Babette's Feast, written and directed by Gabriel Axel (Denmark: Nordisk Film, 1987).

113 *"blue true dream of sky"* E. E. Cummings, "I thank You God for most this amazing," in *Xaipe* (New York: Liveright, 1950).

115 *"You create your life out of the talents you discover. Or not."* Ken Robinson, "Life Is Your Talents Discovered," TEDxLiverpool, YouTube video, https://tinyurl.com/talentsyoudiscover.

Chapter 9: Fear of Not Having Enough

124 *"Men made it. But men can't control it."* John Steinbeck, *The Grapes of Wrath* (New York: Viking, 1939).

127 *"The Maasai of Africa have virtually no cash income"* Ed Diener, "Income and Happiness," *Observer*, April 24, 2005, https://tinyurl .com/dienerhappiness.

130 *"Scholars Elizabeth Dunn and Michael Norton suggest in their book Happy Money"* Elizabeth Dunn and Michael Norton, *Happy Money: The Science of Happier Spending* (New York: Simon & Schuster, 2014).

130 *"Before you can fight, you have to know what you are fighting for."* Naomi Klein, "Demonstrated Ideals," *Los Angeles Times*, April 20, 2003, https://tinyurl.com/knowwhatyouarefightingfor.

134 *"It is said that children in World War II refugee camps"* Dennis Linn, Matthew Linn, and Sheila Fabricant Linn, *Sleeping with*

Bread: Holding What Gives You Life (Mahwah, NJ: Paulist, 1995).

CHAPTER 10: FEAR THAT YOU'LL BE BROKEN FOREVER

143 **"This, I think, is how Etty Hillesum and Viktor Frankl faced the Holocaust"** Viktor Frankl, *Man's Search for Meaning* (1946; repr., Boston: Beacon, 2006); Etty Hillesum, *An Interrupted Life* (London: Picador, 1996).

150 **"supra-personal connections"** Carl Gustav Jung, *Collected Works of C. G. Jung*, vol. 16, *Practice of Psychotherapy* (Princeton, NJ: Princeton University Press, 1966).

151 **"The most helpful archetypal lens for me is fourfold"** Popularized by Robert Moore and Douglas Gill in *King, Warrior, Magician, Lover: Rediscovering the Archetypes of the Mature Masculine* (San Francisco: HarperOne, 1991).

155 **"A wise man once led me in an exercise that he called Crossroads."** Based on leader training work in the Mankind Project, cochaired by Rick Broneic, John Gaughan, and FuGen Tom Pitner, https://www.mankindproject.org.

CHAPTER 11: FEAR OF THE WORLD

163 **"there are two ways to understand the world"** From Steven Pinker's endorsement of Ronald Bailey and Marian Tupy, *Ten Global Trends Every Smart Person Should Know: And Many Others You Will Find Interesting* (Washington, DC: Cato Institute, 2020).

165 **"At any rate, it's still quicker to report looting by a few"** See, for instance, Paul Hawken, *Blessed Unrest: How the Largest Social Movement in History Is Restoring Grace, Justice, and Beauty to the World* (New York: Penguin, 2007).

167 **"It depends on our participation."** Barbara Holmes, "Contemplation and Racism," Center for Action and Contemplation, June 12, 2020, https://tinyurl.com/moralarc.

169 *"Because that vision is so rarely articulated beyond platitudes"* "The King Philosophy," The King Center, https://tinyurl.com/y4vxkns6.

171 *"But the idea that only violence"* See Erica Chenoweth and Maria J. Stephan, *Why Civil Resistance Works: The Strategic Logic of Nonviolent Conflict* (New York: Columbia University Press, 2012).

174 *"the invisible embrace"* John O'Donohue, *Beauty: The Invisible Embrace* (New York: Harper Perennial, 2005).

Chapter 12: Fear of Death

187 *"So tending it is a heroic quest with enormous struggle"* See Peter Kingsley, *Catafalque* (London: Catafalque, 2018).